YEHUDA BAUER is former head of the Institute of Contemporary Jewry, Hebrew University, Jerusalem

The theme of this book is the gradual emergence of the Jewish people from total political powerlessness – a development stretching over nearly 100 years and culminating in the consolidation of the State of Israel. Ironically, as Professor Bauer demonstrates, events during this period stemmed in part from a belief in the 'power' of the international Jewish community that never existed – but that motivated both the Germans and, after the war, the British.

There are three parts to the book. The first deals with a series of lost opportunities to secure the safety of European Jews from Nazi genocide. The second describes the little-known extent of resistance, both armed and unarmed, among Jews in Europe during the second world war. The third covers the events leading to the creation of the State of Israel, including the relatively unrecognized influence of the survivors of the Holocaust.

Professor Emil Fackenheim has written the foreword.

This is a brief but absorbing study by one of the world's great experts on the Holocaust, who has drawn on a huge body of material to depict one of the unforgettable events in recent history from an arresting and unfamiliar viewpoint.

D1225430

YEHUDA BAUER

The Jewish emergence from powerlessness

UNIVERSITY OF TORONTO PRESS
Toronto Buffalo

©University of Toronto Press 1979
Toronto Buffalo London
Printed in Canada

Library of Congress Cataloging in Publication Data

Bauer, Yehuda.
The Jewish emergence from powerlessness.

Includes bibliographical references.
1. Holocaust, Jewish (1939-1945)–Addresses, essays, lectures. 2. Jews–Politics and government–Addresses, essays, lectures. 3. World War, 1939-1945–Underground movements–Jews–Addresses, essays, lectures. 4. Zionism–History–Addresses, essays, lectures. I. Title.
D810.J4B315826   940.53′1503′924   78-25830

ISBN 0-8020-2328-2

ISBN 0-8020-6354-3 pbk.

Contents

Two of the papers in this volume, 'Rescue by negotiations?' and 'Forms of Jewish resistance during the Holocaust', were first delivered as lectures sponsored by the Joseph and Gertie Schwartz Lectures Committee at the University of Toronto in October 1975. The Committee has also assisted in the publication of this volume, and wishes to thank Dr Bernard Avishai who served as editor.

Foreword

EMIL L. FACKENHEIM

What was the Nazi Holocaust? So uncomprehended and incomprehensible is the dread event still, a whole generation after, that in this brief space we can answer this question only with a series of negations.

1 / The Holocaust was not a war. Like all wars, the Roman War against the Jews was over conflicting interests – territorial, imperial, religious, other – waged between parties endowed, however unequally, with power. The victims of the Holocaust had no power. And they were a threat to the Third Reich only in the Nazi mind.

2 / The Holocaust was not part of a war, a war crime. War crimes belong intrinsically to wars, whether they are calculated to further war goals, or are the result of passions that wars unleash. The Holocaust hindered rather than furthered the German war aims in World War II. And it was directed, not by passions but rather by a plan conceived and executed with methodical care, devoid of passion and, indeed, unable to afford this luxury.[1]

3 / The Holocaust was not a case of racism although, of course, the Nazis were racists. But they were racists because they were antisemites, not antisemites because they were racists. (The case of the Japanese as honorary Aryans would suffice to bear this out.) Racism asserts that some human groups are inferior to others, destined to slavery. The Holocaust enacted the principle that Jews are not of the human race at all but 'vermin' to be 'exterminated.'

4 / The Holocaust was not a case of genocide although it was in response to this crime that the world invented the term. Genocide is a modern phenomenon; for the most part in ancient times human beings were considered val-

uable, and were carried off into slavery. The genocides of modern history spring from motives, human, if evil, such as greed, hatred, or simply blind xenophobic passion. This is true even when they masquerade under high-flown ideologies. The Nazi genocide of the Jewish people did not masquerade under an ideology. The ideology was genuinely believed. This was an 'idealistic' genocide to which war aims were, therefore, sacrificed. The ideal was to rid the world of Jews as one rids oneself of lice. It was also, however, to 'punish' the Jews for their 'crime,' and the crime in question was existence itself. Hitherto such a charge had been directed only at devils. Jews had now become devils as well as vermin. And there is but one thing that devils and vermin have in common: neither is human.

5 / The Holocaust was not an episode within the Third Reich, a footnote for historians. In all other societies, however brutal, people are *punished* for *doing*. In the Third Reich 'non-Aryans' were 'punished' for *being*. In all other societies – in pretended or actual principle, if assuredly not always in practice – people are presumed innocent until proved guilty; the Nazi principle presumed everyone guilty until he had proved his 'Aryan' innocence. Hence anyone proving, or even prepared to prove, such innocence was implicated, however slightly and unwittingly, in the process which led to Auschwitz. The Holocaust is not an accidental by-product of the Reich but rather its inmost essence.

6 / The Holocaust is not part of German history alone. It includes such as the Grand Mufti of Jerusalem, Hajj Amin al-Husseini, who successfully urged the Nazi leaders to kill more Jews.[2] It also includes all countries whose niggardly immigration policies prior to World War II cannot be explained in normal terms alone, such as the pressures of the Great Depression or a xenophobic tradition. Hitler did not wish to export national socialism but only antisemitism. He was widely successful. He succeeded when the world thought that 'the Jews' must have done *something* to arouse the treatment given them by a German government.[3] He also succeeded when the world categorized Jews needing a refuge as 'useless people.'[4] (In this category would have been Sigmund Freud had he still been in Austria rather than England; Albert Einstein had he still been in Germany rather than America; Martin Buber had he not already made his way to the Yishuv.) This was prior to the war. When the war had trapped the Jews of Nazi Europe, the railways to Auschwitz were not bombed. The Holocaust is not a parochial event. It is world-historical.

7 / The Jews were no mere scapegoat in the Holocaust. It is true that they

were used as such in the early stages of the Nazi movement. Thus Hitler was able to unite the 'left' and 'right' wings of his party by distinguishing, on the left, between 'Marxist' (i.e., Jewish) and 'national' (i.e., 'Aryan') 'socialism' and, on the right, between *raffendes Kapital* (rapacious, i.e., Jewish capital) and *schaffendes Kapital* (creative, i.e., 'Aryan' capital). it is also true that, had the supply of Jewish victims given out, Hitler would have been forced (as he once remarked to Hermann Rauschning) to 'invent' new 'Jews.' But it is *not* true that 'the Jew [was] ... only a pretext' for something else.[5] So long as there *were* actual Jews, it was these *actual* Jews who were the systematic object of ferreting-out, torture, and murder. Once, at Sinai, Jews had been singled out for life and a task. Now, at Auschwitz, they were singled out for torment and death.

8 / The Holocaust is not over and done with. Late in the war Goebbels (who, needless to say, knew all) said publicly and with every sign of conviction that, among the peoples of Europe, the Jews alone had neither sacrificed nor suffered in the war but only profited from it. As this was written, an American professor has written a book asserting that the Holocaust never happened, while other Nazis are preparing to march in Skokie, in an assault on Jewish survivors. Like the old Nazis, the new Nazis say two things at once. The Holocaust never happened; and it is necessary to finish the job.

I I

In 1961 Raul Hilberg wrote that the Holocaust has not yet been absorbed as an historical event.[6] His statement is still valid. Nor, in view of the particularity of the scandal is this surprising. Still, it does speak poorly for the quality and courage of the academic mind that a famous historian, Arnold Toynbee, was able to say that 'what the Nazis did is not peculiar,'[7] that most other historians of the period devote only footnotes to the Holocaust;[8] that noted psychiatrists apply their neat categories to the victims without looking at the crime;[9] that most Christian theologians ignore the six million Jewish crucifixions at the hands of baptised, never excommunicated Christians;[10] and that philosophers seem to see no significance in the event for their discipline. One of the few to take notice, Theodor Adorno, once observed that whereas the Lisbon earthquake, a merely natural evil, had sufficed to cure Voltaire of Leibniz's theodicy, the 'real hell' of Auschwitz, a man-made evil, was 'paralyzing' the 'metaphysical capacity.'[11] He was promptly rebuked by a German philosopher who announced, in the name of dialectical materialism, that the 'negation' of Auschwitz was being overcome by a 'negation of the negation,' that Auschwitz was a 'turning point,' the 'birthplace of something new, better, higher, more valuable that *must* come after Auschwitz.'[12] One gathers that those 'victims of national socialism who are today achieving the "overcoming" of the past'[13] are none but communists. One also gathers that any philosophical thinking about the unthinkable still necessary is confined to the bourgeois West – that in East Germany the slate is clean. No wonder memorials behind Iron Curtain countries are only to victims-in-general of fascism-in-general. Even in the West, however, the memorials are few, and the best of them are pervaded by a sense of impotence.

Under these circumstances a more than ordinary responsibility rests with the historian. Even his first task – to establish what happened – is beset with enormous difficulties. It is true that we owe vast numbers of documents to the zeal of German bureaucrats. It is also true that, considering the scarcity of their number and their numbed condition, the survivors have left us with an astonishing number of memoirs. However, the Nazi documents are shot through with euphemisms requiring systematic decoding. They also deliberately suppress or distort any signs of Jewish heroism or saintliness. The evidence suppressed or distorted by the Nazi criminals can only partly be supplied by surviving victims; one fact never to forget is that few of the victims survived – and that the memory of most who did not died with them. To get at the plain, undistorted facts is thus a task for generations.

Nor are the difficulties confined to the facts. These latter are in any case never wholly separable from interpretation, needed even for the sifting of the evidence. Interpretation, in turn, is intertwined with explanation, and to explain historical facts is to show how they were possible. At this point, however, we are faced straightway with an ultimate obstacle. To explain the Holocaust is to explain how it was possible. Yet, when faced with the horror of the whole, the mind accepts its very possibility, in the end, solely because it has been actual. This is an obvious circle. It requires the attention not so much of historians as of philosophers of history. Such attention it has yet to receive.

That despite the ultimate obstacle the historian can go on with his task is shown best by already established facts and explanations which are no longer likely to be disputed. Among the facts: the single-mindedness of Nazi anti-Jewish policies, and the callous indifference or helpless numbness (both in retrospect unbelievable) of most of the world's politicians. Among the explanations two should be mentioned. German historians have come to understand the Nazi state as consisting of a dual system, whose inner core (the SS state) manipulated and penetrated the periphery (the traditional bureaucracy, the army, the judiciary, the clergy) and thus was able to achieve ends which it could never have achieved by itself.[14] Jewish historians have seen that the early responses of the Jewish victims were caused, objectively, by impotence and, subjectively, by a humanistic tradition rendering its heirs unable to believe the unbelievable.

It is natural and fitting that gentile, and especially German, scholars should concentrate on the crime, Jewish scholars, on the fate and responses of the Jewish victims. This distinction, however, cannot be made absolute. For gentile scholars to concentrate entirely on the crime would be, however unwittingly, to view the victims as objects only, thereby perpetuating one aspect of Nazi propaganda even while exposing others. For Jewish scholars to concentrate solely on Jewish responses would be, equally unwittingly, to open the doors to a development in which the nature and enormity of the crime is no longer confronted. (Traditionally Jews are prone to divert attention away from enemies responsible for Jewish tragedies – their motives, aims, methods – and on to themselves. Jewish sins are the essential cause, whether understood in a religious framework (disobedience to God, secularism, Zionism) or in a secular one (passivity, religious exclusiveness and fanaticism, anti-Zionism). With this inward turn, and a focusing on religious or secular repentance as the essential remedy, the criminals actually causing the tragedy become secondary or irrelevant. Whatever one may otherwise think of this inward turn, it is inapplicable to the Holocaust.) The pioneer historians on both sides reject the dichotomy referred to. In so doing they uncover for us a fact the significance of which cannot yet be fathomed. Jewish and world history have met a number of times during the four millennia of Jewish existence. They met during the Nazi Holocaust. Never has a meeting been so dark. Rarely has one been so momentous.

III

Yehuda Bauer's *The Jewish Emergence From Powerlessness*, the work of a professional, philosophically reflective historian, arises from all or most of the above considerations and deals with three seemingly diverse subjects. They are diverse only seemingly, for they are united by the theme of the bi-millennial Jewish powerlessness, and the moral and political necessity to end it after the Holocaust. These two aspects – the bi-millennial fact and the post-Holocaust necessity – exist for us who read this book. The book itself, an historical rather than a philosophical work, considers these two aspects in so far as they shaped the lives of those involved in the events.

The work opens with the revelation, almost unbelievable but argued soberly on the basis of the evidence, that some high Nazi functionaries were prepared to let some Jews go, even when the murder machine was working at full speed. (We are left in no doubt that this was due, not to belated twinges of conscience on the part of such as Himmler, but solely to opportunistic considerations, some of them most outlandish.) Then why did the Allied governments involved not rush to take these Jews? The full answer to this disturbing question is not yet available. But two conclusions of this book are not likely to be seriously challenged: the Allies did not place a high priority on Jewish lives; and, left to themselves, the Jewish organizations did not have the power, the influence, or even the funds to act alone. So early in the book, then, two conclusions already emerge: the Holocaust is an event not only in German and Jewish history but also in the history of the world; and, except for Jewish powerlessness, the event could not have happened as it did or even at all. For the reader (who, after all, is a human being as well as a reader) it is impossible not to conclude that something *had* to change; that after *this*, Jewish powerlessness had become intolerable.

But do its past history and present situation – psychological, sociological, political – enable the Jewish people to become intolerant of the intolerable? Bauer turns next to this question in order to probe it at its most extreme point – Jewish resistance during the Holocaust. Citing Henri Michel's definition of resistance as 'maintenance of self-respect ... and [the refusal to] yield to the blandishments of collaboration,' he in passing and almost unwittingly exposes its parochial nature. The definition does apply, of course, within Nazi-occupied Europe. It does not apply, however, to its Jewish victims who were faced not with 'the blandishments of collaboration' but only with unappeasable terror and relentless murder. Should one, then, dispose lightly of resistance under circumstances such as these, as the exception which proves the rule? Should one not instead look for a definition fit for just these circumstances? Indeed, could it be that, here as elsewhere in the case of trials and tests of the human condition, it is extremity that discloses truth?

Searching for just such a definition, Bauer discovers unexpected light in darkness. Jews studied and prayed when these activities were forbidden. At the risk of death they organized social and cultural gatherings. In order to prolong life just a little, they shared starvation rations and engaged in dangerous smuggling. The did all this, as well as shoot back on the rare occasions when weapons and opportunities existed. Bauer draws the conclusion. *When death to body and soul is law, survival in both*, so long as it is practised as a group activity, *is* itself *resistance*. To the world, such Jewish resistance during the Holocaust is a testimony.[15] To the Jewish people, it marks the beginning of emergence from powerlessness.

Bauer's definition of resistance brings him into conflict with Hilberg. (The conflict also concerns the actual extent of armed Jewish resistance. This, however, is secondary, concerning as it does evidence suppressed by German sources and largely come to light only since the appearance of Hilberg's work.) Hilberg defines resistance, with severe restriction, in terms of the ability to use arms, the will to use them, and their actual use. There is an obvious life-and-death question behind Hilberg's severity: how can the remnant of the Jewish people, unable to count on the world and beleaguered still, ensure its physical survival? There is also a life-and-death question behind Bauer's definition. However, this emerges fully only in his third and final chapter, devoted to the dynamics of the national Jewish movement, from the nineteenth century to the founding of the State of Israel.

The Jewish national movement was all along an interplay between two tendencies: the search for physical protection against European antisemitism, increasingly virulent even before the advent of Nazism; and the search for Jewish spiritual survival – the survival of Judaism, Jewish culture, Jewish ideals, and through all these the identity of the people itself. Prior to the Holocaust these two tendencies were often at odds with each other. During the Holocaust, they at times were in outright conflict. (The conflict was absurd when, in the name of socialist universalism, Bundists refused to join a 'merely Jewish' resistance. It was tragic when the Magnes-Buber group wished to limit Jewish immigration to Eretz Yisrael to fifty per cent of the population, obeying a moral imperative toward Palestinian Arabs but violating another toward the Jewish survivors, after the Holocaust homeless still.) However, the chapter, and with it the book, ends on a note sublime enough to transcend, if not tragedy, at least ambiguity and conflict. Conventional wisdom knows of the roles in the founding of the State of Israel played by the fighting groups of the Yishuv, by political Zionism, by the great powers. It was left for this Israeli scholar, himself more than once a soldier for the state, to suggest that the decisive impulse may have come from the survivors. After the catastrophe some, astoundingly, created and joined *Brichah* – a spontaneous immigration movement to the yet unfounded state, labelled 'illegal' because, after what had happened, its members would no longer wait for the world's legal niceties. Only slightly less amazingly, others would not budge from their miserable 'DP' camps, filled though they were with memories of horror, until the state which had become morally necessary would become actual. Rallying all their powers of resistance both physical and spiritual, despite and because of the Holocaust, these weakest of all Jews gave the strongest testimony that this was the *Kairos* for the bi-millennial Jewish powerlessness to end, for a reborn Jewish state after two thousand years of statelessness. It was this postwar act of resistance, Bauer argues, that was decisive in the postwar Jewish emergence from powerlessness. To Jews, it was a testimony to the Jewish ability, spiritual as well as physical, to perform the deed and live with its results. To the world, it was a testimony that the deed is a moral necessity. And thus it came to pass that for a second time in one generation Jewish and world history met when, if but for a moment, politics-as-usual stopped, world conscience awoke and, on the heels of the Holocaust, the State of Israel was born. It was a meeting as momentous as the first. And because it happened our world today is somewhat less dark.

THE JEWISH EMERGENCE FROM POWERLESSNESS

Introduction

The essays in this volume have an underlying theme: the gradual emergence of the Jewish people from total political powerlessness. This development stretches over a period of nearly one hundred years, and culminated, after the Holocaust, in the consolidation of the Israeli State. The decisive transformations in the social and cultural life of the Jews since the late eighteenth century played a role in this evolution. They formed the background to the ways Jews attempted to adapt to the modern world. In the past, religion had been the source of all Jewish self-definition, and peoplehood had been embedded in the tradition. Now, in the late nineteenth century, some Jews began to think of themselves in ethnic categories, and aspired to national status. Forms of identification other than religious ones began to grow.

The world of the late nineteenth century was, moreover, a world of emerging nations fighting for an ever narrower place in the political sun. The new, and often even the old, nations tended to emphasize their own national identity to the exclusion of others. Such preoccupations left the Jews ostracized by the host nation and contributed to their seeing themselves as members of a different group. At the same time, self-examination, or sometimes even superficial knowledge of Jewish traditions, pointed to the conclusion that the Jewish people could claim equal status with those nations that had made important contributions to human culture. Thus, under external pressure, as well as by their own internal metamorphosis, Jews increasingly announced themselves to be a separate entity.

Furthermore, growing nationalism, coupled with economic and social upheavals, intensified something that had long been there, sometimes simmering under the surface: Jew-hatred. It was not the real, historic Jews in their communities, grappling with the ordinary problems of everyday life, that were hated and feared. Rather, it was the Jew as a symbol of evil, cultivated for many centuries by Christianity, which had appropriated this concept from the less virulent anti-Jewish attitude of the Hellenistic world. Christianity, of course, then added the accusation of deicide. It seems that Christian competition with the older, purely monotheistic religion was exacerbated by feelings of guilt deriving from the fact that the Old Testament people had been abandoned, along with the unique moral teachings that had, after all, originally provided Christianity with its ethical basis. The very existence of the Jewish people contradicted, for some, accepted Christian theological dogmas.

Christian antisemitism, moreover, contributed to the development of that racism which concluded that the Jews were the very embodiment of evil. This conviction was strengthened by economic relations. The 'go-between' position of the Jewish middle-class in European capitalism and the economic competition thus generated also engendered the rise of racial antisemitism.

As well, however, the Jews became the victims of their hosts' pent-up hatreds and destructive instincts as a result of that peculiar combination of conspicuousness and powerlessness which distinguished them in different European societies. Jews were not usually in control of the levers of economic and political power; aside from a few Jewish captains of industry or bankers, their share of such power was marginal. On the other hand, they were part of the middle and intellectual class. They were powerless in real terms, but conspicuous as merchants, lawyers, physicians, journalists, and artists. The holders of real power were hidden behind the impersonality of corporations and boards, whereas the Jews belonged to that section of the middle classes which was easily noticed. This was true everywhere, but especially so in Germany and Poland despite vast differences in the social and economic achievement in these countries.

Moreover, Jewish political powerlessness was complete: out of some 250 ministers in German governments between 1918 and 1932, only two were Jews (Preuss and Rathenau), and the defence of Jewish interests was the last thing on their minds. Organized representation of the Jews (mainly the *Central-Verein*) emphasized the unwillingness of the community to engage in any activity in the political arena of the German Fatherland, though it courageously (and unsuccessfully) fought against antisemitism through the dissemination of apologetic propaganda.

The historical identification of the Jews as the symbol of evil (and later, under the Nazis, as Evil itself) meant that the guilt of the persecutors was transferred to the victim; the Jews were identified with that of which their enemies were truly guilty. For example, one of the basic drives of the imperialist regimes of the late nineteenth and the twentieth century was the desire to dominate the world, or as large a part of it as possible. This desire, real enough in the leaderships of the contending states, was imputed to the powerless Jews.

At the beginning of this century in Russia, the incoherent ramblings about the danger presented to the world by the Jews came together in a forgery known as the Protocols of the Elders of Zion. This forgery, a mainstay of rabid antisemitism to this day in Communist and Arab countries, purported to show that the Jews were out for world mastery and intended the destruction of host cultures. The Nazis took over this imagery and we have evidence that they actually believed the Protocols. In their own minds, the real powerlessness of the Jews was a mirage, whereas the mirage – Jewish world government and world conspiracy – was real.

I intend to show that Nazi preoccupation with the power of the Jews was in part responsible for the way in which Nazi policy towards them developed. The possibility of negotiating for the release of Jews, or for their protection, hinged upon the faith of the Nazis in Jewish power and was wholly consistent, paradoxically, with their resolve to 'remove' (*entfernen*) the Jews from their midst. This is the background for the first of the three essays in this volume.

The reaction of the real Jews – not the ones inhabiting the fantasy world of Nazi dogma – was the reaction of people whose traditional belief in a basically moral humanity made it extremely difficult for them to adjust to the monstrous society that Nazism had created. There murder was elevated to a virtue; accepted moral standards were often completely reversed. Jewish reactions to this horror are the subject of the second essay. Some unexpected responses of the Jews may be noted in passing: in spite of their cultural 'handicap' in dealing with such a situation, their period of adjustment was surprisingly brief, and their overall reaction was by and large not that of demoralization but of non-violent and occasionally violent defiance.

The third essay attempts to set Jewish responses to the situation of powerlessness in their historic setting, leading up to the establishment of Israel in 1948. As the Jewish people emerged into the modern industrial age, recognition of their own powerlessness grew. Their subsequent responses were mainly of two kinds: on the one hand, to establish a defensive position from which a modicum of power, relative and modest though it might be, could be exercised; on the other hand, to work toward a revolutionary change in the general society that would obviate the necessity for a specifically Jewish solution to Jewish problems. The former reaction was by and large that of Jewish nationalism, concentrating more and more upon the drive for Jewish political autonomy in Palestine; the latter response, prevalent at first, took the form of identification with universalist aspirations (socialist, communist, or liberal-democratic) and the rejection of specifically Jewish activity. In more recent years, the repeated failure of such universalist approaches has driven most Jews to the presumption that universalistic dreams can become material only as the harmonized relations of national entities.

In the last essay the process of settling Palestine, which began on a large scale about one hundred years ago, may not be sufficiently explored. It should be clear, however, that without the Zionist settlement in Palestine up to and including the Nazi era, the struggle for the establishment of Israel would have been impossible. More than this: the unarmed and, more particularly, the *armed* struggles of the Jews during the Holocaust were often (though by no means always) inspired by the Zionists. Therefore, the history of the Zionist youth movements, and of the pivotal role they played in the armed rebellions under Nazi rule even before the fight for the establishment of the Jewish State, can be explained only if the history of Zionism up to that moment is taken into account.

Finally, these three essays presume that the history of the Holocaust and its immediate after-effects are central to the understanding not only of Jewish history but of the general history of our times. It is said that Jews are like all other people, only more so. Their fate and the attitude of others toward them have become important concerns of the societies in which we live. This has by no means always been 'good for the Jews.' Yet it seems to have become a fact which Jews and non-Jews alike would disregard at their peril.

It is a great honour to contribute these essays in the framework of the Schwartz Memorial Lectures. I would like to thank my good friends, Professors Emil Fackenheim and Michael Marrus, who took care of all the arrangements, and another good friend, Professor Raul Hilberg, who joined Professor Fackenheim and myself in the symposium of October 1975 when two of these three papers were read. Finally, Professor Bernard Avishai did a wonderful job as the editor; his efforts helped transform thoughts and expressions into words I hope are meaningful.

KIBBUTZ SHOVAL
Israel

Rescue by negotiations?
Jewish attempts to negotiate
with the Nazis

Was there a possibility of saving a part of European Jewry, or a significant number of European Jews, by negotiating with the Nazis? Let us try to put the question into a proper phenomenological context by putting it again, and differently: did a willingness exist on the part of Nazis to forego the murder of some Jews, or to let significant numbers of Jews go, and was this willingness conditional? If the latter, which Nazis were willing, under what conditions, and why? When did such willingness become apparent? Were the Allies, were the Jews (or some Jews) aware of such an attitude, if, indeed, it existed? Behind this problem lurks another with far-reaching implications: were opportunities lost to save Jews, and others as well? This essay will attempt to clarify some of these questions.

I shall analyse only a part of the available historical evidence. Four incidents will be chosen: one, the Schacht negotiations with Rublee and the Intergovernmental Committee for Refugees in 1938-9; two, the Working Group negotiations with Dieter Wisliceny in Bratislava, in 1942-3; three, the Kasztner-Brand negotiations with Eichmann in Budapest in early 1944, and the subsequent mission of Brand to Istanbul in May-June of that year; four, the negotiations conducted by Saly Mayer in Switzerland with Himmler's emissary Kurt Becher, August 1944 to February 1945.

The mass of material available to the historian on these subjects is great. My research into the first case has been published in my recent book, *My Brother's Keeper*. I shall base my arguments primarily on this research with an occasional glance to the archives of the German Foreign Office. For the second case study I shall rely on the letters written by Rabbi Weissmandel and Gizi Fleischmann which are contained in Weissmandel's book, *Min Hametzar*, as well as on Wisliceny's own testimony and on German Foreign Office material. For cases three and four I will rely not only on published material, but especially on the Saly Mayer papers (which I discovered a few years ago) now located in New York, supplemented by official U.S. material now available at the Roosevelt Library, Hyde Park, New York.

As we begin to attack this very complex problem, it may be useful to emphasize that the Nazi policy of mass murder of the Jews – I suggest we discontinue the use of the word 'extermination,' a typical Nazi term – developed over a period of some eight years after the takeover in 1933. It seems fairly well established, as Helmut Krausnick has pointed out in his contribution to Buchheim's *Anatomy of the SS State*,[1] that the decision to kill the Jews rather than to expel them was taken not earlier than the period between December 1940 and March 1941. I would tend to fix the date around March 1941, because that is when the other orders concerning the treatment of the civilian population in the forthcoming Russian campaign were issued. Mass murder started with the killing operations in June 1941. Prior to this, during the period 1933-8, promotion of emigration was the favoured policy, and from 1938 through 1940 the Nazis resorted to a policy of *forced* emigration and the theft of emigré property. This latter policy was paralleled by the attempt between October 1939 and April 1940 to establish a Jewish reservation in the Nisko area near Lublin, and thereafter by planning, from July to the late autumn of 1940, for the expulsion of European Jews to Madagascar.

It was in this second period, 1938-40, that the first incident took place. Austria was annexed in March 1938 and 200,000 more Jews consequently found themselves in the Nazi trap. The Roosevelt administration, trying to take the wind out of the sails of its liberal critics, finally determined to 'do something for the Jews.' The American government thus called a conference of over thirty nations at Evian, France, in July 1938. Presidential initiative was limited, however, by restrictionist, isolationist, and even antisemitic sentiment rampant in the U.S., so that any relaxation of American immigration laws for the sake of admitting more Jews was quite out of the question. Had the administration tried to relax these laws, Congress might well have passed even more restrictive ones. Equally, any allocation of government funds for the resettlement of Jews anywhere else would have been politically unrealistic: no U.S. funds were envisaged, for instance, for the ultimately abortive attempts to settle Jews in the Dominican Republic, in British Guiana, and in the Philippines.

Nothing much was achieved at Evian except to establish a new body, the Intergovernmental Committee for Refugees (IGCR). This committee did not even have an administrative budget of its own, yet it was supposed to negotiate with Germany and other countries to ensure the ordered emigration and settlement of 'political refugees' – the use of the word 'Jews' was frowned upon in polite political circles. The IGCR was headed by George Rublee, an American lawyer.

Our story begins when, during the Evian conference itself, a crude attempt was made (we do not quite know by what Nazi authority) to sell Austria's Jews to the West. This attempt, immortalized and needlessly embellished by Hans Habe in his novel *The Mission*,[2] was not taken seriously by the delegates. Rublee nevertheless attempted to convince the Nazis that they should let the Jews leave with some capital in order to make their immigration attractive to the receiving countries.

An internal disagreement then developed in Germany between those, such as Ribbentrop, who wanted to refuse Rublee's advances altogether, and those, like Hjalmar Schacht, who wanted to exploit the mass emigration of Jews for Germany's benefit. Schacht did not believe that the forced emigration of penniless Jews would do Germany any good. He therefore devised a plan which, in its revised version, proposed that 150,000 young German and Austrian Jews would be allowed to leave with one-fourth of German Jewry's capital, all in German goods. They would be followed by 250,000 children and middle-aged relatives after the 'pioneers' had made good. The 200,000 remaining, older people who could not emigrate, would be kept alive with the three-fourths of German Jewry's capital that would have been confiscated by the German State. This plan had the obvious added advantage of promoting German exports by sending abroad many German goods requiring spare parts and replacements. German industry would receive a boost, and the Jews would disappear. Schacht got Hitler's explicit approval for this plan on 2 January 1939.[3] Schacht coincidentally resigned his position as Reichsbank director on 20 January, but his line of policy was adopted by Goering.

In the same month of January, however, the Nazis created the Central Office for Jewish Emigration in order to force Jewish emigration by more brutal means. Emigrants were robbed of their property and then simply expelled. This too, was under Goering's overall supervision, but the actual execution was in the hands of Reinhard Heydrich and the SS. Available evidence indicates quite clearly that both policies had Hitler's approval and were intended to be pursued in a parallel fashion. The Nazi position was, or appeared to be, that if the Jews could be got rid of by bartering them to the rest of the world, this would be acceptable; if the rest of the world did not want them, they would be made penniless and expelled by force.

The Schacht plan involved the establishment of a fund in the free world which would ensure the absorption of Jews into the countries of immigration either by mass settlement in some circumscribed territory, or by infiltration of existing economies. But the U.S. did not want the Jews to come to its shores.

The Roosevelt administration had created the IGCR in order to find a solution that would win for U.S. policy the acclaim of liberals without changing the quota laws or sanctioning the immigration of Jews into its own country. This has been clearly shown by the recent works of Henry L. Feingold, Saul S. Friedman, and David S. Wyman.[4] The administration also balked at the prospect of increased imports from Germany.

Moreover, Jewish efforts at massive fund-raising were feeble, largely because of the impact of the Depression; it was in any case clear that funds for resettling hundreds of thousands of people could not be collected by private agencies. The alternative would have been to ask the administration to provide a large part of these funds. But the Jewish leadership in the United States did not dare to press for money for, as we have noted, it would have been politically impossible for Roosevelt to respond positively.

The British, it is true, in a change of policy in June 1939, suggested that governments provide funds for settling Jews. (Prior to that date they had opposed any idea of governmental support for Jewish emigration.) But the Americans still demurred. Their alternative was to force the Jews, despite all the difficulties, to provide the funds themselves. Consequently the so-called Co-ordinating Foundation, set up in June 1939 by Jewish leaders in the U.S. and Britain at the behest of Roosevelt, was invited to take action. Yet still no governments offered to take large numbers of Jews, and funds were no less hard to come by. The war broke out in September 1939 before anything serious could be achieved.

It seems clear from the evidence that the Nazis were contemplating letting out those Jews over whom they had control – some 300,000 German Jews, 140,000 Austrian Jews, and an unspecified number of people defined as Jews by Nazi laws. To these were added, in March 1939, 115,000 Jews in Bohemia and Moravia. The fact, equally obvious, that this was only one prong of a two-pronged approach – the other being a policy of terror to force out the penniless Jews – does not subvert our conclusion.

It must be admitted, of course, that these plans of Schacht and his successor in the negotiations, Goering's emissary Helmut Wohlthat, involved long-term projects. They counted on an ordered emigration lasting for at least four years in the initial stage, when the young German Jews would leave; the later emigration of adults would take longer. One might therefore infer that Hitler's approval for Schacht's plan was really disingenuous since he was already planning a war. This may be true, but we also know that Hitler was hoping until the very last moment to avoid a conflict with Britain, and that in 1939 he expected the war to be short. The Jewish problem would still have to be solved, as Lucy Davidowicz recently reminded us in *The War against the Jews*, by the eventual disappearance of the Jews (*verschwinden* – another key word in Nazi policy).[5] If the Jews could disappear through a process of emigration by which Germany would gain an economic advantage, so much the better.

The agreement of Hitler to the Schacht Plan appears therefore to be of considerable importance after all. It would indicate that the 'Jewish problem' was far from settled, at least to the extent that Hitler's mind was still not quite made up. His attitude, and that of his immediate entourage, was far from 'immutable' – the German word *unwiderruflich* conveys much more expressively the full weight of the cruel stupidity of this term.

What then aborted the agreement? Undoubtedly it was a combination of factors, but the main one was that the Jewish question simply was not of any real importance to the West, and to Roosevelt in particular. The Jews had no power, no ability, as Coser would suggest, to influence the decisions of others. There was an economic crisis in the U.S. that had deepened in 1938, and mass immigration of Jews was unthinkable. The Daughters of the American Revolution and other patriotic and right-wing agencies had considerably more clout, as Friedman, Feingold, and Wyman have amply demonstrated.

American Jews, moreover, had insufficient money. The total income of the American Jewish Joint Distribution Committee (JDC), dispensing American Jewry's aid to Jews abroad, was $8 million for 1939. About $100 million dollars would have been needed to establish German Jews abroad in addition to the German goods representing the 25 per cent of German Jewish capital that the emigrants would be allowed to take out. The Nazis really believed their own propaganda, as recent works on Hitler and Himmler have made clear, and thought that they were dealing with a satanic force ruling the world of their opponents.[6] They never believed that Jews could not find the funds necessary to secure the emigration of German Jewry. But all this speculation was superfluous. The war had broken out and it was too late.

Still, it should be stressed that emigration of German, Austrian, Czech, and, under certain circumstances, even Polish Jews, did continue in 1940. The numbers were not unimpressive. This clearly indicates that German policy toward the Jews was pursuing parallel lines of emigration and destructive persecution for some time into the war.

We may reiterate, then, that emigration was made impossible, not by the Germans, but by the Allies who seemed to see in the Jews the spectre of 'enemy aliens.' No elaborate negotiations but only common decency would have been sufficient to assist the emigration of very large numbers of Jews to the West during 1940 and well into 1941. Many of these would probably have joined the large numbers of previous refugees who ultimately entered the ranks of Allied armies. More exasperating, no foreknowledge of mass murder, the plans for which did not yet exist, was required in 1940 to stir up such decency. One could merely peruse papers like the *New York Times*, or magazines like *Fortune* and *Life*, to find all the misery, oppression, starvation, and other effects of ghetto life in Eastern Europe graphically photographed and documented.

The orders to stop Jewish emigration from Nazi-controlled territories were finally issued beginning in July 1941. By November of that year all exits, with a few exceptions, were closed. The order for the mass murder had already been given, it seems, by the previous March. Finally, the Jews were facing an 'immutable' decision. Or were they?

There lived in Slovakia a young ultra-orthodox rabbi, a son-in-law of the great rabbi Shmuel David Halevi Ungar of Nitra, by the name of Michael Dov-Ber Weissmandel. When the deportation of Slovak Jews to Poland started with the expulsion of 16-year-old girls in March 1942, Weissmandel got in touch with his former arch-enemies in the Jewish community – the Zionists. It is interesting how in times of extreme crises the old leaders are often shoved aside and new ones capture the initiative. One of these, in her own way as unlikely as Weissmandel, was Gizi Fleischmann, leader of the Women's Zionist organization in Slovakia, hitherto a philanthropic ladies' group. She also represented the American Joint Distribution Committee and its welfare work in Slovakia. Coincidentally she and Weissmandel happened to be related.

Weissmandel and Fleischmann approached the Nazi who was behind the deportations in Bratislava, Dieter Wisliceny, special police attaché for Jewish questions to the German Embassy and an ss man. Parallel attempts were being made to bribe Slovak officials to stop the deportations, but it was increasingly clear that the key lay with Wisliceny. After three months of deportations an agreement was apparently reached in June to pay Wisliceny a sum of $50,000. One half was paid up with great difficulty but it seemed to have an effect: there were no deportations in July and August. In September four more trainloads of Jews were deported to Poland. During that month the other half of the sum was finally collected and paid. The deportations then stopped for almost two years.

Can we attribute this moratorium to the bribe? Weissmandel, furious and despairing, believed so; he accused the JDC and the Jewish world generally of being an accomplice to the murder of the last four trainloads of deported Jews. He charged that the second half of the money had not been paid in time despite appeals to the JDC to send it. He was certain that the $50,000, finally paid and delivered, averted the final destruction of Slovak Jewry for two more years.

Historians until now have tended to discount his view and have attributed the stoppage of the deportations to Slovak second thoughts and competing Nazi priorities of murder. By July 1942 the Jews of the Warsaw ghetto were being murdered en masse at Treblinka death camp: the Nazis, it is said, had no time for small-scale operations such as those from Slovakia.

There is no contradiction, however, between Weissmandel's account and the German documentation, including Wisliceny's postwar testimony. Weissmandel remembered that the whole story began sometime in *Tammuz* 5702, June 1942, when he decided to approach Hochberg, a Jewish Gestapo agent with access to Wisliceny, with the offer of the above-mentioned bribe to stop the deportations. Weissmandel told Hochberg he represented an imaginary world association of rabbis which had close relations with the JDC and could pay in foreign currency. After a short time, Hochberg came back and offered, in Wisliceny's name, the following terms: a cessation of deportations immediately as a sign of good will; the payment of half the bribe after two weeks; a further cessation of deportations for another seven weeks; and the final payment of the other half of the bribe after that. Deportations would then cease completely. The Jews, however, would have to see to it that the Slovaks were bribed as well and did not demand the further expulsion of Jews.

German documents bear out the story. On 25 June Wisliceny and Hans Ludin (the German ambassador) met with the Slovak prime minister, Vojtěch Tuka. The Germans completely surprised the Slovaks by saying that, since 35,000 Jews had been declared by the Slovaks to be economically vital to the country, no more deportations could take place at the moment. Wisliceny would have to go over the protection letters given by the Slovaks to those 'indispensible' Jews before proceeding any further.[7] Actually, nothing like 35,000 Jews had been protected; less than half that number would have been nearer the truth.

Ludin, too, reported to the German Foreign Office that, owing to Church resistance and bureaucratic graft, the deportations would have to be halted. In his postwar testimony, Wisliceny talked of $20,000 that reached him through Hochberg after negotiations in which Hochberg mentioned the name of the 'Joint' (JDC).[8] Wisliceny recalled that this was in September 1942, not June, but the discrepancy may not be important since he had no documents to refresh his memory. He also recalled that he had reported to Ludin and to Eichmann, and had written a report which was finally submitted to Himmler: 'In this report I suggested negotiations with representatives of the "Joint," pointing to the intensive propaganda abroad that would ensue once the Final Solution became known.' He then said that he had managed to convince Eichmann to allow him to stop the deportations until the Church and others calmed down.

This account makes little sense. Once a report had been submitted to

Himmler, it was most unlikely that Eichmann would have given his consent to the cessation of deportations on his own. It would therefore seem that Himmler gave his agreement as well, and that he did so because of the prospect of negotiations with the JDC. Weissmandel put it more intriguingly after the war: 'Apart from the money, they wanted in this way to get in touch with Jews in the U.S., for some political reason that was more important to them than the extermination of Jews.'[9]

Weissmandel, continuing his account, observed that the deportations stopped as promised, and that after the first $25,000 was paid the seven weeks' respite was granted. After that, three more transports were sent to Poland, said Weissmandel, because no way was found to assemble $25,000 more. It was impossible to get this sum from abroad, and Hungarian Jews would not contribute for fear of getting involved with illegal manoeuvres. When, he continued, the other $25,000 was nevertheless collected and delivered, the deportations stopped again (though in actual fact one deportation did take place after the second payment), and were not renewed until 1944.

There is no reason to doubt that additional factors, some of which I have already mentioned, were relevant: the protests of the Vatican, the summer offensive in Russia, the deportations from the Warsaw ghetto, and Slovak fears of retribution after the war. Yet I believe that a connection between the payments and the stoppage of the deportations is undeniable. Indeed, following up Weissmandel's intriguing testimony, the very paltriness of the sums involved seems to point to the possibility that financial considerations were secondary even though foreign currency was involved. The primary considerations may in fact have been political. We shall return to possible political motives later.

In November 1942, Weissmandel again approached Wisliceny, again through Hochberg, and asked what the price would be for a cessation of deportations throughout all of Europe. The question was formulated by Weissmandel himself, written on an old Underwood typewriter on Swiss writing paper and signed by an imaginary 'Ferdinand Roth' in the name of World Jewry. The reaction was quite surprising. Wisliceny took the letter to Berlin, and returned with the answer that the German side was in principle willing to discuss the matter. Negotiations began with the Slovak 'working group'; Gizi Fleischmann and Eng. André Steiner were involved.

We have a series of letters from Bratislava, dated from January to June 1943, enabling us to follow the process of these talks. The Germans finally demanded $2 million and further negotiations – this time with 'Joint' representatives. In return, deportations would stop from the whole of Europe except the Altreich (old Germany), Austria, and the Protectorate (Bohemia and

Moravia). Poland was left out of the discussions by Wisliceny altogether, though the 'working group' kept coming back to the problem of Polish Jews.

On 10 May, the Germans demanded a final answer to their offer within one month. The JDC representative in Switzerland, Saly Mayer, was well aware of the seriousness of the proposal but all his funds were in Swiss banks under rigid war-time controls – and were much less than $2 million. Even had he been able to acquire the sum, he would not have had a way to transfer it to Bratislava. Neither did the New York office of the JDC have the money. In any case, the New York centres of the JDC, the World Jewish Congress, and other agencies, all of whom received information of the offer, did not for a moment believe that it was serious. They did nothing about it. Nor did the Jewish Agency in Palestine, alerted by its representatives in Istanbul, who believed that the offer was serious, have either money or methods of transfer. Desultory talks took place until August 1943, and then Wisliceny told the Jews that the discussions would be, for the moment, halted. He reassured the Jewish negotiators that the Germans might return to them later.

There is absolutely no trace of these talks in any German correspondence. Wisliceny did mention in his postwar testimony the 'Europa Plan' – the name by which Weissmandel and Fleischmann have called the proposals. He claimed that Eichmann submitted the plan to Himmler. Again, Wisliceny would hardly be the man to continue contacts with the Jews on his own so one must assume such contacts were indeed maintained at Himmler's behest. Moreover, the theory that the German proposals were serious appears more plausible against the background of German defeats in North Africa in November 1942 and at Stalingrad in February 1943. According to Weissmandel, Hochberg reported a discussion with Wisliceny in which it was implied that some Germans 'believe that it is within the power of World Jewry to influence the Allies to make peace with Germany in order to fight together against the enemy from the North.'[10]

It seems obvious to me that the SS did not regard the $2 million dollars as anything but an opening gambit for something they really wanted. That objective will be further clarified if we proceed to consider the third incident. This is perhaps the best known of the four, but historical treatment of it has tended to be very uncritical.

Hungary was occupied by the Nazis on 19 March 1944, and some 800,000 Jews were trapped. Eichmann, and his murder squad, the Sondereinsatzkommando, came in immediately. With enthusiastic help from Hungarian antisemites in positions of power, the process of marking, defining, and expropriating the Jews was very swift. Ghettoization began in April, and in May deportations to Auschwitz murder camp had already begun. The whole procedure was executed with such dispatch that no organized resistance took place at all.

An ineffective and submissive Judenrat was set up, based on the prewar Jewish welfare society that was representative of the orthodox and 'neologue'* communities of Hungarian Jews and the Zionist Organization. This more or less reflected the relative strengths of different groups in Hungarian Jewry. However, a parallel organization of the adult labour wing of Hungarian Zionism, a section within a very small Zionist minority, came into existence as well. The leaders of this group were Otto Komoly, head of Hungary's Zionist organization, his deputy Reszoe Kasztner, and the man responsible for illegal operations of the Zionist group, an ex-communist activist of uncertain background, Joel Brand.

As we are not at present concerned with the intricacies of those nightmarish events, I shall simplify.[11] Kasztner, the man responsible for contacts with the Germans on behalf of the Zionist Rescue Committee, knew all the details of the 'Europa Plan' negotiations: Wisliceny had moved to Budapest as a member of Eichmann's murder gang, and had a letter of introduction from Weissmandel to the leader of Hungary's orthodox Jewry. Kasztner tried to exploit these contacts for all they were worth.

The serious bargaining began with Wisliceny for the lives of Hungarian Jewry. Sums of money in Hungarian currency were paid, but there were no results. Eichmann very quickly removed Wisliceny from these negotiations and took over himself. For some reason he preferred to deal with Joel Brand, rather than with the more intelligent Kasztner, and on 25 April he presented his famous offer: a million Jewish lives for 10,000 trucks – which would not be used against the West – and an ill-defined quantity of goods such as coffee, tea, and cocoa.

On 19 May, Brand arrived in Istanbul with this offer. He did not come alone but in the company of a most interesting figure, Bandi Grosz, alias Andreas Gyorgy, to whom we shall soon return. Brand submitted his plan to the Istanbul group of Jewish Agency emissaries who immediately informed the U.S. and British ambassadors in Turkey and the Jewish Agency in Jerusalem. We shall not follow the twists in Brand's dramatic story: his journey to Syria, his imprisonment by the British, and his long talk with Moshe Sharett, head of the Jewish Agency's Political Department. What is of great importance is that the British and U.S. governments were immediately informed. We must remember that this was 1944: a few months earlier, in January, Roosevelt had established the War Refugee Board (WRB) whose task it was to come to the aid of groups, mainly Jews, persecuted by the Nazis. The WRB could, it

*The 'neologue' communities were traditional, not unlike those of the Conservative movement among American Jews today.

was assumed, be counted on in any realistic plan to save Jews. Deportations from Hungary to Auschwitz began, however, on 14 May – before Brand ever left Hungarian soil, a fact which weakened the argument to the WRB that Eichmann's proposals should be seriously considered.

Did Britain and the U.S. in fact take Brand's mission seriously? They did, but only up to a point. It was obvious that one of the purposes of the German offer was to sow distrust between the West and the USSR. The crude intimation that the trucks would not be used in the West was sufficient. To eliminate the possibility of a misunderstanding, the West immediately informed the Soviet Union of the German offer, to which the Soviet deputy foreign minister, Andrei Vishinsky, replied on 18 June: the Soviet government 'does not consider it expedient or permissible to carry on any conversations whatever with the German government on the question touched upon.'

The British government seemed genuinely alarmed that the Americans might seriously consider negotiating with the Germans for the release of Jews. 'There seems to be some danger,' an internal British government report stated on 31 May, 'that an indication that we might negotiate might lead to an offer to unload an even greater number of Jews on to our hands.' The British government indicated to the U.S. authorities on 5 June that the 'implied suggestion that we should accept responsibility for maintenance of an additional million of persons, is equivalent to asking the Allies to suspend essential military operations.' The concessions demanded by Germany, the British argued, seemed calculated to stave off Germany's defeat and were therefore unacceptable. Internal Cabinet Committee discussions in London, moreover, put the word 'rescue' of Jews in inverted commas: the implication was that the proposals were not serious. Any action on behalf of Jews, it was contended, 'would overlook the fact that German brutality has been directed very extensively, above all in Poland, against non-Jews.' These words, by the way, were written by Anthony Eden, who had signed the United Nations declaration of 17 December 1942 that had condemned the singling out of all European Jews for mass murder.[12]

American reactions were more careful. On 9 June the acting secretary of state, Edward Stettinius, was informed by the director of the WRB that Roosevelt himself had 'agreed with our thought that we should keep the negotiations open if possible.' Eichmann's proposals might be 'the forerunner of other proposals.' Negotiations should continue 'in the hope that, meanwhile, the lives of many intended victims will be spared.' This paralleled the policy of the Jewish Agency. Sharett, director of the Agency's Political Department, asked for continued negotiations in order to gain time and lives, though he was aware that no trucks could be delivered to the Nazis. Specifically, the Agency wanted Brand to go back to Hungary with the message that Eichmann's offer was being discussed and further negotiations would take place.[13] The British, surprisingly enough, were in favour of Brand's release from Cairo where he had been detained, but for a number of reasons Brand did not return to Hungary.

Let us now go back to Bandi Grosz. This gentleman, who to this day thrives in southern Germany, is of Jewish ancestry. He worked for the German Abwehr (military intelligence) before the occupation and was ordered to establish contacts with Allied services in Turkey, which he did. He also served the Hungarian military intelligence, and in 1943 he began working as well as a courier for the Zionist Rescue Committee in Budapest. When the Germans occupied Hungary the Abwehr unit in Budapest was liquidated by the SS; so Mr Grosz transferred his allegiance to that organization.

Grosz was well known to the Allied outposts in Istanbul when he arrived there as Brand's companion. He stated the object of his mission at a trial in Israel in 1954 in the following terms: 'My own mission was the main one, Brand's was only a cover.' It consisted of an attempt, in the name of Otto Klages, chief SD commander in Hungary, to make contact with the Western Allies and try to arrange for a meeting between German and American officers to discuss whether a separate peace could be negotiated. Grosz claimed that Klages had told him to conduct this peace feeler very carefully. The best cover appeared to be Brand's offer, since the latter would become superfluous if a separate peace were achieved; the persecution of Jews would cease in either case.[14] Grosz's story was believed by the emissaries in Istanbul, as Ehud Avriel, one of their number, said at the Israeli trial.[15] In fact, the British Foreign Office cabled its embassy in Madrid on 20 July: 'We have secret evidence that the Nazis are using Jews in order to make contact with British and American authorities as a cover for peace proposals with the obvious motive of dividing HMG and U.S. governments from the Soviet government.,[16]

On 6 June, Reuben Reznik, the JDC representative in Ankara, who was attached to the U.S. ambassador there, wrote in a memo that, regarding Grosz (Gyorgy), 'the U.S. Military Intelligence, the American Consulate-General and other allied services have fuller details.' Grosz asked, said Reznik, that any negotiations should be conducted, not by Jewish organizations, but by a representative of the Allied governments. It was likely that a military putsch was being prepared in Germany, and that the Germans were intent on creating a favourable climate toward such an event in the West. In this connection there was a suggestion that Grosz (Gyorgy) may have brought some information regarding such a putsch. He was well known to the Allied secret services, and the peace feelers which he brought with him were taken seriously. Later, when he was in Cairo, Grosz told the full story of his mission to his British interrogators.[17]

Brand himself was aware of the importance of the Grosz proposals, of which he had at least some knowledge. The reports of the Agency emissaries in Istanbul in May and June 1944 leave no doubt about this. I would tend to conclude that Grosz was right: his was the main mission; but the sale of Jews to the Allies would nevertheless have been a good ploy to start the process of negotiation going, and also a political card of real importance. After all, the Jews in the Nazi pseudo-religion fulfilled the role of the satanic force ruling the West and the non-Nazi world in general; if peace with the western Allies was to be obtained, some accommodation regarding the Jews might pave the way.

It is by now fairly well established that Himmler had some prior knowledge of the anti-Hitlerite underground, whose machinations culminated in the attempted putsch on 20 July 1944. Heinz Hoehne, in his book on the SS, provides some convincing evidence that Himmler in fact maintained contact with parts of the anti-Nazi conservative underground though he may not have known the details of the forthcoming assassination attempt.[18] It is open to question whether other central figures in the SS were equally innocent of such knowledge. In any event, accounts such as that of Hoehne, and memoirs such as those of SS intelligence chief Walter Schellenberg or Felix Kersten, Himmler's masseur, suggest that after 1942 Himmler had been playing with the idea of saving Germany by making a separate peace with the West. If that were the case, the Brand-Grosz mission would seem consistent with its German background. Otherwise, the mission is inexplicable.

This leads me into the fourth incident with which I shall deal: the Swiss negotiations. These were a direct consequence of the failed Brand-Grosz mission. The British and American governments did not want to close all doors to possible rescue attempts, largely for fear of public opinion after the war. This point was made, *expressis verbis*, in the discussions of the British Cabinet Committee on Refugees. It is also fair to say that the people in charge of the WRB wanted to do all they could to advance realistic rescue schemes within the framework of conditions imposed by the war. Suggestions were made regarding possible intermediaries. Two persons suggested by Kasztner, a British and an American citizen already accepted by the Germans, were rejected because of apprehension about strong Russian objections.

In the end it was agreed, although with grudging and half-hearted British acquiescence, that Saly Mayer, the JDC representative in Switzerland and a Swiss citizen, should conduct the negotiations. Mayer was a very proper and strictly observant Jew, a respected businessman who was also a former president of the Swiss Jewish community. The WRB drew up instructions for him which were transmitted to Roswell D. McClelland, a former social worker with the Quakers, who served as the WRB representative at the U.S. embassy in Berne. These instructions, bearing the date 21 August and signed by the secretary of state, Cordell Hull, explained that the U.S. government 'cannot enter into or authorize ransom transactions of the nature indicated by German authorities. If it was felt that a meeting between Saly Mayer and the German authorities would result in gaining time, the Board has no objections to such a meeting ... Saly Mayer should participate as a Swiss citizen and not (repeat not) as representative of any American organization.'[19]

What followed, from 21 August 1944, when Mayer met with Kurt Becher (Himmler's emissary) at the St Margarethen bridge near St Gallen, to February 1945, when contacts were broken off, is one of the more remarkable stories of that dark period. In a series of meetings during August and September 1944, Mayer managed to shift the discussion from goods and trucks to ransom money. The fact that he kept the talks strictly secret with no other Jewish representatives participating resulted in his incurring the wrath of the various Jewish groups who were desperately trying to help but were only getting in each other's way.

Mayer far exceeded the terms of his brief. His reports to the man who was supposed to supervise him, McClelland, received the latter's full approval, and the relationship between the two men developed into a warm, personal friendship. But Mayer never told McClelland the full story. He not only talked money to the Germans, but even promised them quite definite sums. Of course, he never hinted to the Germans that he was not empowered to talk to them about goods or money. Nor did he reveal to them that on 8 August, prior even to the talks, he had been told by the Swiss chief of the alien police, Heinrich Rothmund, that the Swiss government would refuse entry to Jews who came as a result of a ransom deal. He never mentioned to McClelland either that he actually bought Swiss tractors and sent them to Germany in order to show the Germans that there was reason to continue the negotiations.

The first result of the Swiss talks was the transfer to Switzerland of a trainload of Jews from Hungary, 318 in number, who were part of a group of some 1690 Jews that had been organized by Kasztner in Budapest in June 1944. The SS agreed to ship these Jews out of their empire, and with this act seemed to commit themselves to further negotiations. It also implied that they might ease the 'immutable' decision to murder all Jews. The release of the 318 had been made a precondition of the first meeting on 21 August. The second group, over 1300 in number, was released in December during the course of further negotiations. It should also be noted that, from the very first, Mayer shifted the discussions from Hungarian Jewry alone to the overall problem of Jews in Europe, and in September began to broach the subject of non-Jewish slave labourers and camp victims as well.

Becher, impressed by Mayer, cabled Himmler a very positive report, hinting that, since a good impression was being made on the Allies via Mayer, the negotiations should be kept up. On 25 August, Himmler ordered the suspension of further deportations of Jews from Budapest; this seems to me to have been a direct result of this development.[20] The Nazi representatives next began to press Mayer for a meeting with someone who would have political plenary powers (*mit allen politischen Vollmachten*). Mayer, without money, without backing, but with an urgent desire to keep the discussions going, asked the Nazis to specify what they would want to buy with the money he would give them in Switzerland. An SS emissary by the name of Herbert Kettlitz was sent to Switzerland to find the goods in the small, beleaguered, shortage-ridden country. It was obvious that he had no idea what he wanted, and that the real purpose of the Nazis was different: Becher wanted to meet an American with political authority. Mayer would have to produce McClelland if the negotiations were to continue.

Becher's second in command, Max Grueson, told the leader of Hungarian orthodoxy, Philip von Freudiger, that the purpose of the Germans was 'to urge the Jews who, it is notorious, control all operations in Britain and the U.S., to compel the Allies to stop the war against Germany. Germany would be ready to undertake a common action with the western powers against Russia.'[21] Becher himself was given the opportunity of proving to his boss, Himmler, that his contacts with Mayer did, in fact, lead to the U.S.

On 5 November, a unique event took place in the history of World War II: SS-Colonel Kurt Becher, on direct instructions from Himmler, met in Zurich with Roswell D. McClelland, attaché to the U.S. embassy in Berne. At that meeting Mayer demanded an end to the killing of all civilians, Jews and non-Jews, intervention by the International Red Cross, and the exit of orphans to Switzerland[22] – the Swiss had finally agreed to that.

In October and November 1944, Himmler gave first oral and then written instructions to stop the gassings at Auschwitz. It is impossible to determine the immediate motives for this decision: obviously the impending collapse of the eastern front, the growing desire to look for an alibi, and other factors all were involved.

But when all is said and done it would appear that the Mayer negotiations played at least some part in Himmler's decision. The collapse of Nazidom, rather than leading to the order to stop the gassings, could well have produced the opposite reaction: the Jewish remnant might have been destroyed, quickly and radically, in order to eliminate all witnesses to Nazi crimes. Murdering did not cease, of course: overwork, freezing, starvation, and indiscriminate shooting destroyed many thousands of human lives. But the gassings stopped.

As I have already stated, we know today what Mayer did not know until early 1945: Himmler himself was the force behind Becher and was personally guiding the negotiations. Himmler protected himself by obscuring the purpose of the negotiations, and by presenting them to Hitler and Ribbentrop as a deal which would bring Germany and the SS much needed materials in return for the release of some Jews.

We also know that Hitler himself had given his half-hearted agreement to such a course in July 1944. As Ribbentrop reported: 'The Fuehrer has decided, upon my suggestion, to accede to the wishes of the Hungarian government in the question of offers from abroad to ship Jews there.' (*Der Fuehrer auf meinen Vorschlag entschieden hat, der ung. Regierung in der Frage der auslaendischen Angebote fuer den Abtransport von Juden ins Ausland entgegenzukommen.*)[23] Himmler's purpose was obviously different, but he had to show some real gains in money or goods before any further steps could be contemplated.

On 21 November however, a State Department cable arrived in which Edward Stettinius forbade any deal in which the WRB would agree to pay ransom, and refused Mayer's request to transfer $5 million to Switzerland for Mayer's use in the talks. Mayer succeeded in bluffing his way through nevertheless, and Becher, in the mistaken belief that the money was forthcoming, advised Himmler to show good faith. Again, the progress of the negotiations explain some further SS 'gestures.' On 6 December, the rest of the so-called Kasztner transport of about 1300 Jews was released from Bergen-Belsen and arrived in Switzerland. Also consider the following: Eichmann had started to deport Jews from Budapest by foot-marches to the Austrian border. During the month of November, tens of thousands of Jews were marched under the most frightful conditions; very many died. But at the end of November, an order was given to halt the foot-marches. It seems likely that the hope of achieving something in the Mayer negotiations contributed to this SS decision.

In early January, the opposition of Stettinius to the transfer of $5 million to Mayer was finally overcome. The money was not paid to the Germans, but served only to goad the SS into further talks. There were now also parallel efforts through other intermediaries: the Swiss politician Jean-Marie Musy and, in Sweden, a Nazi by the name of Peter Kleist who tried to contact the Americans there.

As the end of the war drew nearer, Himmler's efforts to arrive at a separate agreement with the West grew more and more frantic. Surviving fragments of Himmler's correspondence bear this out. On 15 January 1945, he finally asked: 'Who is it that the American government is really in contact with. Is it a Rabbi-Jew or is it the Jioint?(sic)' (*Wer ist derjenige mit dem die amerikanische Regierung wirklich in Verbindung ist. Ist es ein Rabbiner-Jude oder ist es die Jioint?*).[24] The SS leaders who survived the war all testified that Himmler tried to prevent the actual mass murder of the remaining Jews, an attitude towards which the Mayer negotiations probably contributed. As a consequence, some 150,000 or 200,000 Jews were liberated from the concentration camps when the war ended.

Many more, of course, did not benefit from the decline in mass killings: they were tortured to death, marched to death, shot, or succumbed to the effects of starvation and disease. It would be wrong, furthermore, to depict Himmler as a late convert to humanity; but he did try to save his own skin. Incredibly, he seemed to think that the West might see in him a leader of some postwar Germany allied to it in its struggle against Russia.

To conclude then, however much this conclusion is at odds with conventional impressions, a willingness *does* appear to have existed on the part of the Nazis to let significant numbers of Jews go – for a political price. This willingness is naturally much more pronounced after El Alamein and Stalingrad, and it became positively urgent as the war approached its end. But even before the war itself, and certainly before the decision to murder all Jews was taken, some key Nazi figures were prepared to exchange Jews for political and economic advantage.

Which Nazis were willing to let the Jews go? Paradoxically, the very people who executed Hitler's order to kill them: Himmler and a certain group of his closest associates – Schellenberg, Wolff, and Klages.

Why were they willing? For the war period, this question can be answered quite easily. They believed the Nazi theory that the Jews, a demonic force, were running the world; in an attempt to strike a compromise with the West the European Jews in SS hands thus might be key hostages (*Faustpfand*), compelling the Western powers (under their Jewish dominance!) to come to terms with an SS-run Germany. This aim – trading the Jews for a political settlement – did not contravene the Nazi determination to get rid of the Jews, expressed by Himmler as late as April 1945 in his talks with the emissary of the World Jewish Congress from Sweden, Norbert Mazor. The SS leadership saw itself still loyal to Nazi ideology when it tried to stop the war and, at the same time, get rid of the Jews by expulsion. In fact, Himmler was consciously following a policy that had, in January 1939, received Hitler's explicit approval.

Why not return to the Schacht-Goering line if Germany stood to benefit from it? Some Allied, and some Jewish, leaders were at various times aware that the expulsion option was serious, and, although nobody could foresee in 1939 that Jews left under Nazi rule were under so pervasive a sentence of death, everybody could see that they were faced with a single-minded persecution.

Were the possibilities of saving Jews exploited? In 1939 the problem was how to save 600,000 German and Austrian Jews. An effort was needed but there was no incentive for the Western powers to make it. How many battalions, in Stalin's famous phrase, did the Jews have? They would have to support any anti-Nazi coalition anyway: they were in the bag, for the little they were worth. A humanitarian gesture toward them was all that could be expected – that gesture was made through Rublee – but when this gesture threatened to become a commitment to accept refugees, the problem was handed back to the Jews themselves.

The Jewish organizations in 1939 were powerless. More than this, they had no understanding that the Schacht proposals were an alternative to, at best, more brutal expulsion. They were divided into warring factions and they had nowhere near the required funds. Nor were they equipped to raise even insufficient funds.

The Allies saw the Jewish problem as a side-issue of the war. The Russians refused even to consider it. Britain was afraid that the Jews would be unloaded on her, or that the prosecution of the war might be affected. I would even claim, on the basis of the British documents I have seen, that a good deal of antisemitism, quite openly expressed in internal discussions, entered into the British stand. The Americans, for their part, wanted to help, especially after the establishment of the WRB. But they would have nothing to do with ransom negotiations, since they too were afraid of Russian reactions.

During the war itself the Jews were quite ineffectual. They could not openly criticize the Allies. They had little money, and less influence. It was only tenacious and courageous individuals, such as Weissmandel, Kasztner, and Mayer, who grasped the awful situation and rescued – through bluff and pretence – as many Jews as they did, and more than could have been expected.

There was a possibility of saving Jews by negotiations; no historian can say how many. A Hebrew saying goes: 'He who has saved one human life is likened to him who saved an entire world.' Many worlds were needlessly lost. The conclusion that negotiations might have secured the survival of very many Jews is inescapable; but to save them would have required other priorities, a change in thinking and purpose, on the part of the Western Powers and the public opinion that supported those governments. Given the context in which the leaders of the West operated, no such rescue was possible. This demonstrates how cheaply human life is valued in civilizations confident of their humanism.

Forms of Jewish resistance
during the Holocaust

We have already seen that the basic situation of Jews during the Hitler period was one of political powerlessness. Negotiations to save them, if conducted at all, would have to have been supported by one or more of the major
powers; without that there would be little chance of success. Jews could appeal to the powers, they could try to impress public opinion in the Western
democracies, but in the end they were perilously dependent upon the mercy
of others. In the free world, Jews could appeal or beg for help; behind the
barbed wire of Hitler's hell they could cry out in the hope that muted echoes
would reach the outside. Was there anything more that the trapped Jews of
Europe could do? If so, did they do it? What was the reåction of the victims to
the most terrible terror any regime had yet exercised?

Jewish reaction to Nazi rule is of tremendous importance to Jews and non-
Jews alike. The Jew wants to know the tradition to which he is heir. How did
that tradition, that whole range of historically developed values, stand up to
the supreme test of Hitler's death sentence on the Jewish people? Did Jewish
civilization, demoralized under the blows of the brutal enemy, surrounded in
the East by largely indifferent or hostile populations, simply collapse?

These questions are equally significant for non-Jews. Nothing like the Holocaust had happened before, but there are no guarantees against its recur-
rence. Jews are not the only possible victims of genocide. It is urgent to know
how people react in such extreme circumstances; to find out how people, who
were Jews, reacted when it happened to them.

What do we mean by resistance? What, more specifically, do we mean by
that term in the context of World War II? What, when we apply it to Jews?
Henri Michel, perhaps the most important contemporary historian of anti-
Nazi resistance, defines the term negatively: resistance was the maintenance
of self-respect. He writes that 'acceptance of defeat whilst still capable of

fighting, was to lose one's self-respect; self-respect dictated that one should not yield to the blandishments of collaboration.'[1] But it is practically useless to analyse Jewish resistance with such categories – the Nazis certainly did not use the blandishments of collaboration on the Jews.

Professor Raul Hilberg, on the other hand, seems to regard armed resistance as the only, or nearly only, legitimate form of real resistance. In his monumental book, *The Destruction of the European Jews* (Chicago, 1961), he stated categorically and, to my mind, mistakenly, that the lack of Jewish armed resistance to the Holocaust was a consequence of the fact that Jews during their long diaspora had not had occasion to learn the art of self-defence.[2]

Let me start off with a definition of my own and we shall then subject it to the test of known facts. I would define Jewish resistance during the Holocaust as any *group* action consciously taken in opposition to known or surmised laws, actions, or intentions directed against the Jews by the Germans and their supporters. I cannot accept Michel's definition because there were in fact very few Jews who consciously collaborated with the Germans, or who were willing to help Germany achieve victory in the hope that they would help themselves or the Jewish people. There were, of course, paid Jewish Gestapo agents and others who helped the Germans having been promised their lives – quite a number of these. But I know of only one clear and one marginal case of collaboration as defined here: I am referring to the group known as the 13 (*Dos Dreizentl*) of Avraham Gancwajch, in Warsaw, and to Moshe Mietek Merin's Judenrat in Zaglębie.

I cannot accept Hilberg's definition or description for two reasons. In the first place, I do not think he is being historically accurate. Jews did defend themselves throughout the ages by force of arms when this was feasible or when they had no other choice – in Polish towns against Chmielnicki's hordes in 1648; in Palestine against the Crusaders; in medieval York. One could cite many such instances. In pre-1939 Poland, moreover, the socialist Bund party had special defence groups that fought street battles with antisemitic hooligans. Early in this century, Jewish students in Prague, Vienna, and Berlin established fraternities that fought duels against antisemites, and so on.

The second and more important point is surely that armed resistance during the Holocaust was possible only under conditions that most Jews did not enjoy. You either have arms or you do not; for the most part, the Jews did not. Still, the nature of Jewish armed resistance was much more complicated than one might expect.

In the Generalgouvernement (the central area of Poland ruled by the Nazis) there were, according to exhaustive historical accounts,[3] about 5,000 Jewish fighters. Of these about 1,000 fought in the Warsaw ghetto rebellion, 1,000 in the Warsaw Polish uprising in 1944, and the rest as partisans in forests and in a number of ghetto and camp uprisings. There were some 1.5 million Jews in the area in 1939, so one gets a ratio of resisters of 0.33 per cent – not a very high figure – and concludes that Jewish armed resistance was marginal at best. In eastern Poland, where there were about one million Jews before the war, 15,000 armed Jews came out of the forests at liberation – a ratio of 1.5 per cent – which will still not cause one to change the verdict. But during the time Jews were organizing to fight, that is in 1942 and 1943, they accounted for one half of all the partisans in the Polish forests. The other half, about 2500, were Poles. There were more than 20 million Poles in the Generalgouvernement, so one arrives at a resistance ratio of 0.0125 per cent. The same game can be played regarding other nations in Nazi Europe. One begins to appreciate Mark Twain's adage that there are lies, damned lies, and statistics.

Let us then disregard such futile exercises and examine the real facts concerning Jewish armed resistance in Poland and, subsequently, elsewhere. It is generally accepted that large-scale operations were mainly dependent on two ingredients: the availability of weapons, and the support of a civilian population capable of aiding underground fighters. Neither of these preconditions existed for the Jews. Jews did not have access to the arms buried by the collapsing Polish army in 1939. There were very few Jewish officers in that army, fewer of them holding high ranks (e.g., one general), and the secrets of the buried arms were kept by right-wing officers who went into hiding.

The Polish government underground, the Armia Krajowa (AK), did not buy any arms from deserting German soldiers until very late in the war. No partisan detachments of any importance were established by it before 1943, and, anyway, not only were Jews not accepted in AK ranks, but a number of AK detachments were actively engaged in hunting down and murdering them. Thus when the Jews realized that they were being threatened with mass murder in 1942, there were no AK detachments for them to join. When these did come into existence, most Jews had already been murdered, and the detachments, in any case, would still not accept the survivors.

The Communist Gwardia Ludowa, later the Armia Ludowa (AL), was founded in the spring of 1942. It was then very weak, had very few arms, and about half its partisan forces were in fact the Jewish detachments in the forests of the Lublin area and elsewhere. By the time the AL grew stronger (in 1943) large numbers of Jews were no longer alive, but survivors did join the AL. Its weapons were bought or captured from peasants or, in most cases, parachuted by Soviet aircraft.

Jews locked in ghettos generally had no way to procure arms. The AK would not provide them; the Communists still did not have them. Controls at the gates were so strict that it was virtually impossible to bring any arms that could be obtained into the ghetto. The best known exception to the rule was in Vilna where Jews worked in German armouries. There, despite very stringent security measures, arms were smuggled into the ghetto from the city. The same general conditions applied in Czestochowa, which explains why the underground there had secured arms despite the obstacles.

Let us now turn to the three basic scenes of armed resistance in the east – the ghettos, the forests, and the camps. In the ghettos, the Jewish population was starved and decimated by disease and forced labour. They were, moreover, surrounded by a gentile population whose reaction to Jewish suffering varied between indifference, mostly hostile, and open enmity toward the victims. As applied to the ghettos Hilberg's thesis seems correct, that so long as the Jews thought they would survive the Nazi rule and the war they could see an incentive to re-enact the modes of passive conduct that in the past had tended to ensure the survival of the community, and they were accordingly reluctant to engage in armed resistance.

Resistance would have met with the disapproval, not only of the Polish population, but even of the Polish underground, the AK. Stefan Rowecki, commander in chief of the AK, issued an order (No. 71) as late as 10 November 1942 which bluntly stated that 'the time of our uprising has not come.' He mentioned the fact that the 'occupant is exterminating the Jews,' and warned his people not to be drawn into a 'premature' (!) action against the Germans.[4]

An examination of ghetto armed underground organizations shows quite clearly that, indeed, the Jews entered into the phase of practical preparations for armed action only *after* the first so-called *Aktion*, i.e., mass murder operation by the Nazis. Ghetto rebellions never took place when a hope of survival could be entertained – only when the realization finally struck that all Jews were going to be killed anyway. All other armed rebellions during World War II were predicated on the assumption that there was some chance of success. In the ghettos, no such success could be contemplated; the only result of ghetto rebellion would be the annihilation of all Jewish residents and the subsequent plundering of the empty Jewish houses by the surrounding population – that is, when the Germans did not plunder the houses themselves. This plunder, by the way, ensured the cooperation of the local population in the murder of the Jews and also prevented the escape of survivors: the local population had a strong incentive to ensure that no witnesses survived.

By the time of the first major waves of Nazi murder in 1942, only a small remnant (some 15 to 20 per cent) of the Jewish population still lived in the ghettos. This remnant then had to form an organization which might either be opposed by the Judenrat or, if the Judenrat supported a rebellion, would have to coordinate its plans with the latter in some way, and would have to secure arms in the face of supreme difficulties. In the western and central part of Poland, moreover, there were no forests where partisans could hide, so that escape was impossible. During the summer of 1942 the Warsaw underground did send Jewish groups into forests some distance from the capital, but the hostility of the Poles, the murderous actions of the AK, and German patrols quickly put an end to these attempts.

The situation was different in the eastern parts of Poland, western Byelorussia, and the eastern parts of Lithuania. Here the forests were thick, but in 1942 and early 1943 very few Soviet partisan groups were operating. In Minsk, where there was a ghetto of 84,000 Jews, the Judenrat led by Eliahu Mishkin was part of an underground movement which tried to smuggle Jews out to the forests. Some arms were obtained, luckily, for the few Soviet partisans in the area would not accept Jews without them. But only a small number of persons could be suitably equipped from among the many who were sent out. In the city itself no effective non-Jewish underground was organized for a long time and no help was obtained from the Byelorussians; on the contrary, the ghetto had to hide anti-Nazis who could not hold out in the city. We do not yet know how many Jews were smuggled out to the forests from Minsk; we are working on a list, and it will take a long time yet before the job is finished. But I would guess the number to be between 6,000 and 10,000. About 5,000 survived the war in the forests – which shielded only those bent on escape and capable of bearing arms.

I should now like to address another problem: collective responsibility. The Nazis murdered a great many persons in retribution for the rebellious acts or suspected sedition of the few. In Dolhynov, near Vilna for instance, two young men who were about to leave the ghetto for the forest were caught, but managed to escape and hide. The Germans told the Judenrat that if these men did not return and surrender, the ghetto would be annihilated immediately. The two men refused to return, knowing that they were endangering the lives of hundreds of others. On the morrow the inhabitants of the ghetto were shot. What would we have done in the place of the youngsters?[5]

Yet the main internal problem for the Jews was not that of the collective responsibility imposed upon them by Nazi reprisals so much as the more fundamental problem of family responsibility. To belong to a resistance group one had to abandon one's family to death – not just leave it at some risk, as with the non-Jewish resister. The young Jewish man had to make the clear-cut decision to leave his parents, brothers, sisters, relatives, and sweethearts, and watch them being transported to death while he stood helpless, albeit wearing the mantle of the resistance fighter. Abba Kovner, the great Israeli poet and former head of the FPO (Farainikte Partisaner Organizacje), the resistance movement in the Vilna ghetto, has told how he gave the order to his people to assemble at an appointed hour: they were to leave the ghetto through the sewers in order to continue the battle in the forests. When the time came, and he stood at the entrance to the sewer, his old mother appeared and asked him for guidance. He had to answer her that he did not know. And, said Kovner, from that time on he did not know whether he deserved the prestige of a partisan fighting the Nazis or the stigma of a faithless son.[6]

Let us then recount, in the face of these facts, what the armed resistance of Jews in the East amounted to. In the Generalgouvernement there were three armed rebellions, at Warsaw, Czestochowa, and Tarnów; four attempted rebellions, at Kielce, Opatów, Pilica, and Tomaszów Lubelski; and seventeen places from which armed groups left for the forests, Chmielnik, Cracow, Iwanska, Józefów, Kalwaria, Markuszew, Miedzyrzec Podlaski, Opoczno, Radom, Radzyn, Rzeszów, Sokolów Podlaski, Sosnowiec, Tomaszów Lubelski, Tarnów, Wlodawa, and Zelechów.

There were moreover rebellions in six concentration and death camps – Kruszyna, Krychów, Minsk Mazowiecki ('Kopernik'), Sobibor, and Treblinka, together with the famous Jewish rebellion in the gas chambers at Auschwitz in late 1944. These were the only rebellions that ever did take place in any Nazi camps, except for that of Soviet prisoners of war at Ebensee at the end of the war. There were armed international undergrounds, in Buchenwald and Auschwitz for instance, but they never acted. (In Buchenwald they took over the camp after the SS withdrew.)

We know also of 30 Jewish partisan detachments in the Generalgouvernement, and a further list of 21 detachments where Jews formed over 30 per cent of the partisans. These latter groups were all part of the AL, because, as I have explained, the AK wouldn't accept them. Individual Jews fulfilled important functions in the AK, but they had to hide their Jewishness and appear under assumed names. A further 1,000 Jews participated in the Polish Warsaw uprising of August 1944. The total number of these fighters was about 5,000, of whom over 4,000 were killed.

The situation in Lithuania, eastern Poland, and Byelorussia is much more complicated, and I cannot render a complete picture. At least sixty ghettos had armed rebellions (such as those in Tuczyn, Lachwa, and Mir), attempted rebellions (as in Vilna), or armed underground movements which sent people to the forests (as in Kovno, Zetl, and so on). In some ghettos resistance took more than one form, as in Nieswiez, where an armed rebellion was followed by an escape to the forests.[7] An estimate of Jewish partisans in this area is most difficult to make, though, again, we are currently working on a list. We know that there were some 15,000 Jewish partisans in the area towards the end of the war, and many more must have died before that. Some 2,000 Jewish partisans in the Tatra mountains of Slovakia must be added to any account dealing with eastern Europe.

Two further points. First, the problem of defining a 'Jewish partisan' is no simple matter. Do we include in that category only Jews who fought in Jewish groups? Or may we include Jews who fought as individuals in non-Jewish groups, such as Soviet partisan units? Moreover, what about Jews who denied their Jewishness and fought as Poles, or Russians? There were, after all, a number of communists (such as Yurgis-Zimanas, the commander of the Lithuanian partisans) who emphatically defined themselves as Soviet or Polish citizens, specifically denying their Jewish backgrounds. This is also true of a few Jews in the AK, and of some of the central figures in the AL command. But these cases were generally few and far between, for Jews were required to identify as such, irrespective of their particular political ideology. Indeed, the attitude toward Jews who refused to identify as anything but Poles or Soviets was often negative in character, so that one is left to wonder whether there is any justification for excluding even communist leaders and assimilationists from an analysis of Jewish resistance. Were not their individual idiosyncrasies overwhelmed by the intruding fate of the Jewish community to which they perceived themselves to belong only by birth?

Second, we cannot ignore antisemitism even in the Soviet partisan detachments, especially those in which Ukrainian partisans had great influence. A large number of such cases have been documented, as have the fatal consequences for a number of Jewish fighters. This hatred was directed not only against Jewish units – which the Soviet partisan command disbanded – but also against individual Jews in general units. Where there were large numbers of Jews in some unit, a struggle against antisemitism was likely; but in smaller detachments with relatively few Jews, defiance was much more difficult.

Let us also deal, albeit summarily, with western Europe. Here the story is less dramatic, first, because the total number of Jews in France, Belgium, and Holland was less than one-sixth of the Jewish population of prewar Poland and, second, because armed resistance movements of a serious kind did not become active until well into 1943. By that time there were not many Jews left to fight. In the west, of course, the same hostility towards the Jews did not exist as in the east, but there were notable exceptions. In France, for instance, the French police effected most of the anti-Jewish measures. There were Jewish armed groups in the OJC (Organisation juive de combat) and the MOI (a communist group) in France, two groups in Belgium, and two communist groups of Jews in Germany. By and large, however, Jews participated as individuals in non-Jewish organizations because no ghettos were set up in western Europe. Should we consider them as Jewish resisters, or as Belgian and French resisters?

I think the answer depends on the way these Jews acted. Was their behaviour more likely the result of specifically Jewish concerns or not? The answer is important because it would help us to measure the depths of Jewish identification among western Jews. It would also help to reveal the extent of integration among Jews and non-Jews. We are still in the middle of these researches, but I would venture the general conclusion that these Jews were usually fighting for 'Jewish' reasons.

How many Jews fought? In France there were thousands rather than hundreds and there were probably close to a thousand in Belgium. Moreover, the Jews were usually the first to act – for example, the first urban guerillas fighting against the Nazis in Paris during the spring of 1942 were members of a Jewish unit of the pro-communist MOI. The Guttfreund group in Belgium took up arms as early as September 1941, killing a Jewish Gestapo agent, robbing a factory producing for the Germans, and later burning a card index of Jews at the Judenrat offices in Brussels. Finally, thousands of Jews fought in northern Italy in 1943-4, and thousands more fought with Tito's army in Jugoslavia.

Let me summarize: Jewish armed resistance was considerably more widespread than has been subsequently assumed. In eastern Europe, a high proportion of those who survived the first wave of murders participated in armed activities. Jewish rebellions in Warsaw and elsewhere were the first urban struggles against the Germans anywhere in Europe, and the Jewish rebellions in the camps were the only ones of their kind. Michel's conclusion that Jewish armed resistance was proportionately higher than that of other people, with few exceptions, is probably true. This is remarkable in light of the greater difficulties Jews encountered and of their lack of modern military tradition. Surely the radical nature of the Nazi threat to Jewish communities is pertinent here. But persecution does not explain resistance, especially when the former is attended by elaborate forms of control and coercion. At any rate, it seems easier to explore the ways Jews in Palestine and then Israel met their military challenges in the light of the above analysis than to believe, with Hilberg, that there was little struggle in Europe and then a sudden inexplicable upsurge of martial skills that enabled the Jews of Israel to fight for their existence.

I have dealt with armed resistance first because unarmed active resistance is best explained against the background of armed struggle. Let us now therefore consider the problem of resistance without weapons.

Unarmed struggle took place largely before the murder actions began. In such situations, when Jews were unaware of any Nazi intentions to murder them, Jewish behaviour was at least in some measure comparable to the behaviour of non-Jewish populations under Nazi rule. Such comparisons are important as measuring-rods for the behaviour of populations subject to the rule of terror. On the other hand, differences between Jewish and non-Jewish situations will stand out clearly as time moves on, and we cannot avoid approaching both comparable and noncomparable situations with the knowledge that the Jews were later subjected to Holocaust, whereas other nationalities were not.

What, then, did these other subject nationalities in Europe do? Did they obey German law, even those laws forbidding education in Poland and Russia? Yes, they did. Did they resist the shipment of slave labour to Germany? No, they did not.

By and large the Jews, on the other hand, proved recalcitrant. History had taught them the art of evasion, and they showed themselves to be highly skilled practitioners. In the first place, contrary to conventional wisdom, most German and Austrian Jews, some 410,000 out of 700,000, did manage to leave the Third Reich. (Some of these, tragically, were caught again as the German armies advanced.)

In Poland, after the war had begun, German rules were so brutal that, had the Jews passively acquiesced – even though every infringement of Nazi law was punishable by death – they would have died out in no time at all. Let me give a few examples. Official German food allocations distributed by the Warsaw Judenrat came to 336 calories daily in 1941. It is unlikely that the Warsaw Jews could have survived longer than a few months on such rations. But smuggling, illicit production on a considerable scale, and great inventiveness produced an average of 1125 calories daily. Unfortunately, a large population of unemployed Jewish refugees who had been expelled by the Germans from their homes in the provinces into Warsaw slowly died because their food supplies fell below that average. Many others managed to survive on these rations nevertheless.[8] I would consider this stubborness, this determination to survive in defiance of Nazi authority, to be an act of resistance under the definition I offered at the beginning of this essay. In Kovno, similar smuggling was organized by groups that were controlled by the Judenrat and the Jewish police – the police here were the very heart of the armed resistance organization. It was thus an organized act, under public supervision of sorts, and the aim was very definitely to subvert German laws.

Consider the question of education. Until the late autumn of 1941, education of any kind was forbidden in Jewish Warsaw. But it took place clandestinely, in so-called *complets* where small groups of pupils would meet either in the soup kitchen or in the home of the teacher. We find evidence for this, in fact, in a large number of places in Poland. There were also clandestine high schools in Warsaw which received some funds from illegal JDC (American Jewish Joint Distribution Committee) sources. The activities of such schools are documented. Their older students passed official matriculation exams under conditions which were, to put it mildly, unusual.

Also, according to Ringelblum, there were in Warsaw alone some 600 illegal *minyanim*, groups of Jews praying together throughout the period when all public religious observance was forbidden.[9] Political parties were of course proscribed, as were newspapers or printing of any description. But we now know of more than fifty titles of underground newspapers in Warsaw alone, and most of the political parties continued their clandestine existence.

There is, one is inclined to think, something typically Jewish or – more profoundly – *traditionally* Jewish, in the importance that cultural institutions achieved in such a time. There was, for instance, YIVO, the Yiddish Scientific Institute in Vilna, where Kovner and the poet Abraham Sutzkever were active in preserving materials, establishing a library system, and encouraging literary output in a conscious effort to maintain morale. It was no accident that the YIVO group was a recruiting ground for FPO, the resistance movement in Vilna. The most famous of these cultural institutions was the Oneg Shabbat group in Warsaw. Founded and headed by Dr Emmanuel Ringelblum, the historian and public figure, it methodically assembled reports and diaries and initiated research in order to preserve documentary evidence of the life of the Jews in the Warsaw ghetto. Among its studies were the famous medical investigations into the effects of hunger on the human body under the direction of Dr Milejkowski, which were published after the war in 1946 in Poland.

Oneg Shabbat did not know of the speech in Poznan in 1943 in which Himmler boasted that nothing would ever become known of the Final Solution. But the basic idea of Oneg Shabbat was that knowledge and documentation were forms of defiance of Nazi intent. In this the group succeeded. Despite the fact that only two-thirds of the Oneg Shabbat archives were found after the war, they are our main source of knowledge regarding Jewish life in Poland during the Holocaust.

Of all active unarmed resistance, most intriguing, I believe, were the activities of the 'Joint' (the Joint Distribution Committee), the American-based social welfare agency. The Joint was actually just an office which, in Poland, distributed American funds to local Jewish agencies such as TOZ, a health agency, Centos, a society for the care of orphans, Cekabe, a network of free-loan banks, and Toporol, a society for agricultural vocational training. On the face of it, nothing more tame could be devised. But when war came the Joint offices in Warsaw happened to be headed by a group of men with leftist political convictions, among whom Dr Ringelblum is perhaps the best known today. They very early on realized that it would be their job to fight against Nazi-imposed starvation, humiliation, and gratuitous cruelty.

Until the end of 1941, certain sums still arrived from America through a complicated transfer system; although no dollars were actually sent to Nazi-controlled territory, German marks left behind by Jewish emigrants were sent to Warsaw from Berlin and Vienna. This stopped in December 1941, and the Joint became an illegal institution. But even before this, additional funds were being obtained by illegal means. In 1941, the Joint fed 260,000 Jews in the Generalgouvernement, including some 42,000 children.[10] Centos and TOZ, which had themselves been declared illegal, still maintained their operations under the cover of an official welfare organization. Kitchens and children's homes became the centres of illegal political activities, including party meetings, clandestine presses, and illegal schooling. All this was consciously activated by the Joint.

Parallel to this was Joint support for so-called house committees, of which over 1,000 existed in the ghetto of Warsaw. Residences in eastern Europe were usually built around a courtyard, so that in each instance the 'house' included four apartment buildings, about 200 or 300 families. These groups of people organized spontaneously, outside any Judenrat groupings, to institute mutual aid, schooling for children, cultural activities, and so on. (Unfortunately these groups included Warsaw Jews only; the refugees, crammed in their shelters, were dependent on the woefully insufficient feeding of Joint soup kitchens which were meant to provide only supplementary nourishment.) The house committees sprang up from below, but the Joint quickly realized their potential and Ringelblum set up a roof organization called Zetos. This body tried to create a central fund through which more affluent house committees would help the poorer ones, and encouraged activity essentially opposed to the Judenrat. The steering committee of Zetos became the political base for the resistance movement. The Joint was also behind the preparations for the Warsaw ghetto rebellion, and financed the uprising to a large degree. Giterman, the Joint's chief director, also helped to finance resistance movements in Bialystok and elsewhere by sending them money explicitly for this purpose.

The Joint's was a mass activity which embraced hundreds of thousands of Jews. Still, it obviously could not stand up to the forces of mass murder. Giterman was killed on 19 January 1943 in Warsaw, and Ringelblum was murdered in March 1944 when the Germans finally found his hiding place. They shared the fate of the millions whom they had tried to feed, encourage, and lead. But we cannot be concerned here with their ultimate fate; we are concerned rather with their behaviour prior to their murder. We want to know how widespread was unarmed active opposition to Nazi rule among the Jews; and we discover that owing to the work of men like Ringelblum and Giterman the range of such resistance was considerable.

Let us now very briefly touch upon the question of the Judenraete, the Jewish Councils nominated or approved by the Germans. It must be stated at the outset that their behaviour cannot be subsumed under any generalization. Minsk, which I have mentioned, was not the sole example of Judenrat defiance. Other councils tried to stand up to the Germans and their members were murdered as a result. Still others tried to find a way round German regulations, and managed to survive for a time: the Judenraete of Kovno, Siauliai, Siedlce, Kosow, Piotrkow Tribunalski, France, Slovakia, and other locations belong to this category. Some Judenraete obeyed German commands, but within that framework tried to help their communities. A typical example of this was the Warsaw Judenrat under Adam Czerniakow, who in the end committed suicide rather than be responsible for handing Jews over to the Germans for killing.

A final group consisted, I would submit, of those who saw no alternative but complete submission to the Germans, including the handing over of Jews to the Nazis for deportation, even after there were no illusions about the consequences. Such were the Judenraete of Lodz or Vilna or Lublin. But in the case of Lodz and Vilna submission resulted from the conviction that the only way for a *part* of a community to survive was by doing the Germans' bidding and performing slave labour for them. In the case of Lublin, no policy at all was followed – only terror and frightened submission. There was in fact no Judenrat whose policies, attitudes, and actions quite equalled those of another. However, we find resisters among Judenraete as groups and among Judenrat members as individuals in a fairly large variety of cases.

I have dealt with eastern Europe; but it would be wrong to disregard the 500,000 Jews of western Europe, or indeed the Jews of Germany, Austria, and Czechoslovakia. The Joint, Zetos, and various cultural institutions could be classified as self-governing institutions interposed between the Judenrat and the Jewish masses. Similar groups and organizations existed in western and central Europe as well.

Take for example the OSE.[11] This was a general Jewish health organization which had a rather modest branch in prewar France. During the Holocaust, OSE became the main child-care organization in the Jewish sector. In France, of course, the gentile population had a much more positive attitude toward Jews than that which prevailed in Poland. German rule was comparatively less oppressive; Nazi police and SS were less numerous, while German Army interests, which did not always parallel those of the SS, were more important. In this climate OSE and some other groups managed to hide about 7,000 Jewish children, some in Catholic and Protestant institutions but mostly among peasants, and we do not know of one single case where children were betrayed by those undertaking to hide them. OSE, the Jewish Scout movement, and some other groups managed to smuggle some 2,000 people into Switzerland and a smaller number into Spain. In Belgium, the Comité de défense des juifs, headed by a Jewish member of the Belgian underground, hid thousands of Jews as well.

Let us now turn, very briefly, to what is probably the most important, but also the most diffuse, form of resistance: that of popular, mass reaction. Here we are on uncertain ground, because this form barely comes within our own definition. Can one speak of an unorganized, spontaneous action of Jews as expressing true resistance to Nazi enactments?

Well, up to a point it seems one can. Let us cite a few examples. In Holland, which had a Judenrat of the Lodz type, the Jewish proletariat of Amsterdam reacted forcefully in February 1941 to provocations by Dutch Nazis. A Dutch Nazi died in the scuffle, and Jewish and non-Jewish inhabitants of the Jewish quarter chased the Nazis out. This was the immediate cause for the famous strike of Dutch workers in support of the Jews. It failed, largely because of the intervention of the Jewish leaders who were told by the Nazis that, if the strike did not stop, large numbers of Jews would be taken to concentration camps and killed. The Dutch desisted, and the same Jewish leaders became the nucleus of the Dutch Judenrat. But what should concern us here is the popular Jewish reaction, especially since the story of the anti-Nazi acts in Amsterdam had further instalments.

Nazi documents record that after the first deportations from Holland in July 1942, the Jews ceased to appear at the appointed time and place when called. From the summer of 1942 on the Nazi and the Dutch police had to ferret the Jews out. This was popular unarmed resistance. We know, of course, that this tactic did not succeed; but the measure of resistance is not its success but its incidence. Was the moral backbone of the Dutch-Jewish population broken? It appears, rather, that their desire to live as free human beings was maintained.

Turning to the east, let us inspect another example. The so-called Slovak National Uprising broke out in the hills of Slovakia in August 1944. The Jews from some Slovak towns and camps fled there in large numbers. Those who could, fought; those who could not tried to hide. As the German troops advanced into the Slovak mountains suppressing the uprising, the Jews refused to obey Nazi orders and certainly avoided concentrating in places where they could be picked up by the Germans. This was typical unarmed resistance.

Some of the popular mood of this kind of resistance is captured in diaries which have survived: the young boy who believes that his father is being taken away and will not come back but writes that he believes his own place is with his father; the young man who jumps out the window of the deportation train only when he is already separated from his mother, whom he had not dreamed of leaving to face her fate alone; Chaim A. Kaplan, in Warsaw, who is sorry he will not see the Nazis' downfall which he is sure will come. Such acts and sentiments are beyond our definition of resistance, to be sure; but they form the background to those acts of unarmed circumspect defiance which I have tried to relate.

Let us not exaggerate. There were communities that collapsed. One cannot even find the dignity of quiet defiance in some Jewish responses. In Copenhagen, for example, the whole Jewish community was saved without its lifting a finger to help itself; in Vienna, but for a few hundred people in hiding, nothing but abject submission was the rule. Unfortunately it is impossible to explore here the reasons behind this apparent lethargy.

The range of Jewish resistance was broad, as I have shown: armed, unarmed but organized, semi-organized or semi-spontaneous. Let me conclude with a form of resistance which I have saved to the last because it is the most poignant. My example is from Auschwitz, and I am relating it on the authority of the late Yossel Rosensaft, head of the Bergen-Belsen Survivors' Association. Yossel was also a 'graduate' of Auschwitz, and he testified that in December 1944 he and a group of inmates calculated when Hanukka would occur. They went out of their block and found a piece of wood lying in the snow. With their spoons, they carved out eight holes and put pieces of carton in them. Then they lit these and sang the Hanukka song, 'Ma Oz Tsur Yeshuati.'

None of the people who did this were religious. But on the threshhold of death, and in the hell of Auschwitz, they demonstrated. They asserted several principles: that contrary to Nazi lore, they were human; that Jewish tradition, history, and values had a meaning for them in the face of Auschwitz;

and that they wanted to assert their humanity in a Jewish way. We find a large number of such instances in concentration and death camps. Of course, there were uncounted instances of dehumanization in a stark fight for survival: bread was stolen from starving inmates by their comrades, violent struggles broke out over soup, over blankets, over work details – struggles which only too often ended with death. In the conditions of the camps, incidents of this kind are not surprising or unusual, but examples such as the one mentioned are. The few Jews who did survive could not have done so without the companionship and cooperation of friends. And friendship under such conditions is itself a remarkable achievement.

I think the story of Kosów is also appropriate. It exemplifies most vividly the refusal of so many Jewish victims to yield their humanity in the face of impending murder. Kosów is a small town in eastern Galicia, and it had a Judenrat which was not very different from others. On Passover 1942, the Gestapo announced it would come into the ghetto. The Judenrat believed that this was the signal for the liquidation of the ghetto, and told all the Jews to hide or flee. Of the twenty-four Judenrat members, four decided to meet the Germans and offer themselves as sacrificial victims – to deflect the wrath of the enemy. With the ghetto empty and silent, the four men sat and waited for their executioners. While they were waiting one of them faltered. The others told him to go and hide.[12] The three men of Kosów prepared to meet the Nazis on Passover of 1942. Was their act less than firing a gun?

Zionism, the Holocaust, and the road to Israel

In this essay we shall try to follow the historical currents that led Jewish national movements to seek political power in the form of the Jewish state and also as Jewish pressure groups in the Diaspora. In order to do so, we shall first analyse the roots of the powerlessness from which these national movements tried to escape. That is, we shall isolate their desire to achieve a measure of political power from other no less important aspects of their struggle. There is of course the danger of distorting the picture by emphasizing that which tended to remain obscure. But if Jewish demands for power were not obvious, this may be ascribed to a traditional Jewish de-emphasis on secular political power. Yet it is precisely this historical aloofness that makes the Jewish emergence into the world of political power all the more important.

The term itself and its derivatives – i.e., political power, or its opposite, powerlessness – are here understood as the capability to influence decisions of others, either through the implied or explicit threat of sanctions or through the promise of political advantages deriving from military, economic, electoral, or other assets. We will therefore first examine the evolution of the Jews' determination to achieve political power and some of the background from which it sprang. Then we will deal rather more intensively with the period in which the struggle for political independence reached its apogee, 1945 to 1948. In this period the trends outlined in the first part were most decisively manifest and culminated in the establishment of Israel.

I

It is well known that, since the 'Emancipation,' a considerable number of Jews have spurned specifically Jewish aspirations, claiming citizenship in a rather nebulous internationalism. Unfortunately, modern internationalist movements did not reciprocate; ultimately they would not agree to make Jews equal to others in their scheme of things. Antisemitism was widespread among liberals in Germany, France, and elsewhere, while left-wing antisemitism resulted in increasingly hostile attitudes of the communist world to Jews.

On the other hand, there was a growing disillusionment among many Jews with such purely universalistic approaches to their dilemmas; and this in turn contributed to the increasing identification of the Jewish people with their own civilization and a desire for some kind of political autonomy. This is all the more understandable considering the cultural wealth of traditional Jewish life from which modern Jewish nationalists freely drew, and the world climate in which a large number of peoples from remote corners of the world, and well-integrated minorities in the West (such as the Welsh and Scots), were demanding, and increasingly obtaining, recognition of a separate national status.

While it is true to say that modern forms of Jewish nationalism – the Zionist movement and others – can be viewed as a Jewish reaction to the rise of the national movements which spread from central to eastern Europe in the second half of the nineteenth century, it would be a mistake not to take into account also the deep attachment which the Jewish people traditionally have had to their ancestral Land of Israel. This land was part and parcel of their religious and ethnic consciousness before the modern age, and Jewish attachment to it was undoubtedly the background for the peculiar forms which Jewish nationalism assumed in the modern era.

Indeed, the Jewish connection to Eretz Yisrael never lapsed. A large section of the Jewish population of Palestine were not exiled after the destruction of the Second Temple in 70 CE, and their numbers and importance diminished only gradually under external pressure. Jews have repeatedly attempted to regenerate themselves in Palestine ever since. In 614–17 CE, a Jewish force participated in the Persian conquest of the country and were promised the right to rebuild the Temple. Jews defended Palestinian towns against the medieval crusaders together with their Moslem neighbors. Resettlement attempts were also made in the sixteenth century. Another attempt by the 'false Messiah,' Shabbatai Zvi, to lead the Jewish people back to Palestine failed in 1666, although the readiness of hundreds of thousands to follow him had been made evident.[1] In the hills of the Galilee, uninterrupted Jewish occupation of villages from Roman times to the present testify to the strength of Jewish attachment. Jerusalem, Safad, Hebron, and Tiberias had significant clusters of Jewish population prior to Zionist settlement. In fact, Jerusalem has had a Jewish majority ever since the first population counts were made there in the mid-nineteenth century. The tradition of settlement in the land was a pillar of Jewish self-understanding upon which modern Zionism, whether religiously orthodox or secular, was built.

Modern Zionism and other forms of Jewish nationalism rose also as a reaction to the many-sided antisemitism which developed in the nineteenth century. Contemporary research tends to emphasize that nineteenth-century antisemitism was a continuation of earlier kinds of Jew-hatred,[2] albeit in a much more acute and concentrated form. Religious antisemitism long had existed in both Christian Europe and the Moslem world. In Christianity, its chief expression was the accusation of deicide compounded by persistent rejection of Jesus' redeeming mission. At least in the first centuries of the Christian era, moreover, Judaism was rightly viewed as a dangerous, proselytizing competitor in the pagan world. A typical product of Christian Jew-hatred was the blood-libel, according to which the Jews used the blood of Christian children for ritual purposes.

The particular importance of this medieval superstition lies in the fact that it formed a bridge between 'old' and 'new' forms of antisemitism. Imported from Europe, it served Arab antisemitism as well, as in the Damascus blood-libel accusation of 1840.[3] It was the subject of court proceedings in the Beiliss trial in Russia in 1913. It was levied against Jews in Germany and Austro-Hungary at the end of the nineteenth century, and was finally revived by Nazi propaganda. It even survived Hitler and became the immediate cause of an anti-Jewish pogrom at Kielce in Poland on 4 July 1946, causing a mass flight of those Jewish survivors who had remained in eastern Europe after World War II. This mass flight, by the way, had an important place in the developments leading to the establishment of Israel. Building on this religious Jew-hatred, on xenophobia, and also on economic competition resulting from the Jews' middleman position in the economic and social structure of premodern times, newer forms of antisemitism developed.

This 'new' antisemitism resulted in part from the nineteenth-century awakening of the nations of eastern and central Europe to their national culture and traditions and their consequent recognition of the Jews as a group different from their own. Those emerging nations aspired to establish independence over the largest possible territory and turned against national minorities inhabiting the areas involved. Attempts were made to denationalize such minorities, to make them part of the majority culture. Even liberal nationalists who might have wished to grant minority rights expected minority communities to conform to a state or national culture as defined by the majority people. In the case of Jews this nationalist posture, exacerbated by long-established religious prejudices, brought forth demands that the Jews accept the majority culture, including the majority religion, or emigrate. Hungary, Poland, Rumania, and even some central and western European states manifested this kind of attitude in the late nineteenth and early twentieth centuries.[4] Equal rights were perfunctorily granted, but a tacit and later explicit assumption was made that sooner or later the Jewish citizens would become part of the majority group and give up their specific culture.

The nationalist component of the 'new' antisemitism was compounded by socio-economic ones. The introduction of modern industrialization increasingly deprived the Jews of their pre-modern economic position in eastern European society – that of middleman and artisan. At first, many Jews were pushed into the ranks of the new industrial working class. Many others emigrated to the Americas or, to a lesser extent, to western Europe, and there too they started off in working-class occupations. However, from the earlier twentieth century on, a countervailing process became very apparent, both in the New World and the Old: Jews rose into the middle classes and the free professions. In no country did they become economically powerful enough to wield real economic clout, but since there were a few Jewish captains of industry and banking, and since Jews generally occupied that middle range of economic positions which brought them into direct contact with consumers (as retailers, wholesalers, etc.) they became highly 'visible.' This peculiar combination of apparent economic influence with actual powerlessness made them the butt of economic competition and resentment, and, more important, transformed them into ideal scapegoats in times of crisis. Economic competition was particularly acute in countries such as Russia, Poland, or Rumania, where a national middle class developed only to find that its functions were already being preempted by the Jews. The scapegoat pattern based on economic competition appeared virtually everywhere, however, including North America in the twenties and thirties.[5]

These many strands of modern antisemitism were spun together by a new racist Jew-hatred (as opposed to hatred motivated by religion or economic competition) that culminated in Nazism. In fact, it was the first rumbling of racist Jew-hatred that spawned the misleading term 'antisemitism' with which we are now so familiar. When Wilhelm Marr introduced the term in the 1870s, his purpose was to provide what was then a 'hygienic', scientific-sounding name for Jew-hatred, as Emil L. Fackenheim has pointed out.[6] Racist antisemitism needed such a term because it was based on a quasi-scientific insight into the development of humanity. Perverting the scientific theories of Darwin and his followers regarding the evolution of the species, racism argued that an eternal struggle persisted between human societies, a struggle which would be decided by racial characteristics. 'Better' races were destined to conquer, rule, and even annihilate lower races; their superiority was contained in 'blood.'

The idea of blood as the carrier of race was a perversion of earlier notions which saw in blood the symbol of life and spirit. Racism developed the notion that blood was, not the symbolic, but the actual content of race-determining characteristics. Blood could be mixed by miscegenation between races; but it would thereby become 'impure' or 'bastardized', so that the chances of survival in the eternal struggle for supremacy would be undermined.

Racial antisemitism absorbed virtually all the earlier forms of Jew-hatred within itself. From Christian antisemitism it took over the image of the Jew as the devil – not as the symbol of the devil, as in earlier times, but as the devil himself. The blood-libel fitted particularly well into the new dogma which depicted blood as the carrier of race and the Jew as the corrupter of racial purity. Nationalist antisemitism, economic competition, and the scapegoat syndrome were also woven into the picture of Jews as the anti-race. Hitler himself saw the Jew as a parasite who, if he succeeded in conquering the world by purposeful intermarriage and bastardization of the superior races, would in any case destroy himself as well as humanity – because parasites, Hitler insightfully concluded, are incapable of any life on their own.[7] The Jews were evil, that was clear. They had to be removed, isolated, or expelled. Ultimately, this conviction opened the way for their physical annihilation.

One may reiterate that the racist antisemite tended to transpose onto the Jew that for which he or she was guilty. If ever devils appeared in human form, and displayed unbridled quest for world domination, the Nazis did. Yet their movement professed fear of devilish Jewish domination as the central component of their anti-religion.

There was yet another phenomenon to which Jewish nationalism responded. As the hold of religion over people lessened throughout the nineteenth century, many Jews either watered down their Jewish identity – became citizens of the 'Jewish persuasion' by removing all vestiges of a national separateness from their Jewish religion – or they abandoned Jewish identification altogether. Yet while the assimilation of individual Jews was possible and many Jews continued (and still continue) on this path, the Jewish people as a whole, paradoxically, found absorption into the host society difficult, if not impossible. Jews tended to concentrate in middle-class and intellectual occupations. And the more they tried to move away from established centres of Jewish population in the course of their upward mobility, the more they found themselves in new clusters of Jewish population, for other groups of the host civilization would move away as the Jews moved in. Jews thus became acculturated, they acquired the language and some or most aspects of the host culture, yet they remained separate.

At times, during periods of liberalization, pressure and opportunity for assimilation increased so much that the very survival of the Jewish people seemed to be brought into question; nor did Jewish survival always seem to be particularly desirable to the Jews themselves. But whatever their intentions, economic and nationalist pressures such as those outlined above inevitably caught up with the Jews and underlined their separateness nevertheless. As we have seen in the cursory introduction to this volume, this situation contributed to the determination of many Jews to seek a way back to their own heritage, whether religious or secular, and to rejoin those who had never abandoned it. Theodor Herzl was himself a good example of such a person.

Jewish nationalism was thus an outcome of both external pressures and of a continued, strong Jewish identification deriving from the Jews' religious-ethnic culture. One manifestation of such national sentiment was the slowly evolving desire to create some base for the exercise of political power which would extricate the Jewish people from their peculiar dilemmas.

The term 'Jewish nationalism' has been used without defining it; what is meant by it? I would argue that all movements presuming the continued existence of a Jewish people and trying to find a collective place for it in the modern world should be understood as part of the Jewish national trend. Up to the Holocaust, one could count the Jewish Socialist Workers' Party (Bund), the Folkists, the various groups of Territorialists, and even the ultra-orthodox Agudat Israel as expressions of Jewish nationalism, though some of these would have shuddered at the description.[8] The Zionist movement, which developed from being one of a number of trends and finally became the preeminent – and now practically the only – expression of Jewish nationalism itself embodied many conflicting tendencies. However, all nationalist groups had in common a desire for Jewish vitality and *political* security though they differed widely in their analysis of Jewish needs and in their consequent strategies.

The Agudat Israel, operating in eastern Europe between the two world wars, tried to find a *modus vivendi* with the nationalist regimes of eastern Europe based on the Jews' special cultural-religious needs. In return, the Aguda would support those regimes and exercise a policy of neutrality in the political struggles within the countries in question. Political security was to be bought at the cost of withdrawal into the shell of orthodox, pre-modern Jewish existence. Powerlessness was thus accepted as a fact and as a basis for accommodation with the gentile state – until the coming of the Messiah.

The Folkists dreamed of establishing Jewish national-cultural autonomy in the countries of eastern Europe. Before, and mainly after, World War I they proposed to trade Jewish electoral support for the guarantee of national rights, especially with regard to schooling and the use of the Yiddish language. They assumed that a democractic system of government would endure in eastern Europe and that within such a system Jewish electoral power could be used to guarantee collective rights.

'Cultural' Zionism, as taught by Ahad-Ha'am (Asher Ginzburg), had a great deal in common with this quest for Jewish autonomy in the Diaspora. Ahad Ha'am thought that a small Jewish centre in Palestine would be the source of Jewish cultural inspiration for all of the Diaspora. Late in his life – he died in 1927 – he added that the centre in Palestine would have to comprise the majority of the population in that country; still, he did not believe in the possibility of concentrating the majority of the Jewish people in Palestine. Their interests in the Diaspora would somehow have to be protected. The idea of using Jewish electoral power was therefore by no means foreign to Zionism in the Diaspora, and between the two wars a valiant attempt was made in Poland by leaders such as the Zionist, Yitzhak Gruenbaum, to force the increasingly antisemitic regime to respect Jewish national minority rights by an alliance of the Jews with other national minorities.

Another expression of the quest for a national solution was that of the Territorialists. They wanted the threatened Jewish groups to concentrate in some new territory of their own. Palestine, they thought, could not be secured and some empty territory elsewhere would be preferable: Grand Island in New York State (as proposed by Emanuel Noah early in the nineteenth century), or the Argentine (as suggested by Baron de Hirsch), or western Australia, Angola, British Guiana, or even Galveston, Texas. Herzl's proposal to establish a settlement of Jews in Uganda belonged to this set of projects. Herzl saw Uganda as a 'night asylum' for European Jewry until Palestine became available – but then, so had Noah with his 'State of Ararat' on Grand Island. All these plans aimed at a measure of political security and political power by territorial concentration.

They failed for two reasons. First and foremost, the transformation of Jews from an essentially middle-class urban group to a pioneering community settling a new country could not be achieved without some compelling emotional commitment. The traditions of the Jewish people are far too closely bound up with the Land of Israel to allow for substitutes. Second, the lands proposed were not really 'empty,' even where they were sparsely populated. They were in every case already marked as targets for expansion, liberation, or conquest by some other group or political entity. Of course, Palestine was not 'empty' either; but it was, after all, the ancient homeland.

Territorialist solutions to the problem of Jewish homelessness were considered by communists as well. Communist opposition to Zionism flowed naturally from Marx's rejection of the Jews as a people and his characterization of them in some of his writings as but a symptom of capitalist society that must vanish with capitalism itself. To this ideological inheritance, Russian communism grafted notions which derived from the traditional antisemitism of the Russian intelligentsia. These elements found their concise expression in Stalin's *Marxism and the National Question* (1913), an exposition full of analytical blunders. Its basic error was the limiting of the national designation to groups that possessed four narrowly circumscribed characteristics: one language, a territory, a common economy, and a common cultural background expressing itself in national character traits. Pre-modern ethnic units were 'peoples' or 'tribes' rather than nations. Thus, for instance, the Indian nation, which speaks many languages, would be disqualified as a nation; Austrians and Germans would perforce become one nation because they speak the same language, have the same cultural background, and occupy contiguous territories. Even more important, perhaps, religious and psychological factors, as well as other social dynamics, were ignored. A solid, deterministic framework was created that allowed no elasticity.

Although his booklet was supposed to be devoted to the national question generally, Stalin devoted a major part of it to the Jewish problem. He predicted the ultimate disappearance of the Jews. The progressive elimination of religion as a distinguishing factor meant, Stalin argued, that only the remnants of psychological traits would distinguish the Jews in the future. Jews had no single language, and no territory or area of economic development. The Zionist attempt to recapture some outdated historical reality, to recreate 'artificially' a people that was disappearing, could be termed reactionary. The real task of Jewish revolutionaries, said Stalin, lay in advancing the cause of international revolution by merging with it. There is no doubt that the communist belief in the international revolution was an example of an intense pseudoreligious devotion. In that sense, Stalin's demand that the Jews discard their Jewishness in favour of a communist internationalism can be seen as a demand to the Jews to convert to another religion, thus paralleling similar challenges during the Middle Ages in Christian Europe.

It will of course be noted that Stalin's definitions differed from those of Marx. Marx did not treat the Jews within the framework of the national question at all. His awareness of the national problem generally was rudimentary, and the Jews for him were a phenomenon provoked by capitalism which would disappear with the passing of the capitalist system. Stalin and Lenin on the other hand dealt with the Jews and their relationship with the surrounding world as part of the problem of nationalism with which they had to contend. Lenin himself had met a form of Jewish nationalism in the Bund during the early years of the twentieth century. The Bund, though violently anti-Zionist, demanded the right of autonomous Jewish organization within the framework of a unified Russian Social-Democratic Party. It also demanded cultural autonomy – i.e., the use of Yiddish, and popular Yiddish literature and arts in schools and other Jewish cultural institutions. Jews were a distinct 'people,' and were to be recognized as such in any internationalist, socialist society. Lenin dismissed the Bund as nothing but a Zionist group with a propensity to 'sea-sickness' – Jewish nationalists who did not want to go to Palestine.

When the communists came to power in Russia, many former Zionists and Bundists joined the Communist Party in the hope that the new society would eliminate antisemitism and provide that measure of security which they had sought through their former allegiances. The Jewish Section of the Communist Party (the Yevsektzia) was set up (it existed until 1930), and although it attacked all other forms of organized Jewish endeavour, especially in the capitalist countries, it tried to develop a specifically Jewish identification which would contribute to the general effort of building socialism in the Soviet Union. Non-Jewish communists in Russia early on sought to establish a Jewish settlement on a definite piece of territory despite the initial opposition from the Jewish Section and its newly-converted Jewish communists. Through Kalinin, the venerable president of the USSR, the Party tried a number of times to create in Russia an autonomous Jewish region. In the twenties, under Pyotr Smidovich, a vice-premier of the Russian Soviet Republic, close settlement of Jews in areas such as Kherson and – mainly – the Crimea was advanced. It was hoped that if the Jews attained a majority there, a Jewish national territory would subsequently be set up within the framework of the Soviet Union. Four autonomous Jewish regions were in fact created.[9]

More importantly, from 1928 on the Soviet government began to advocate the creation of a Jewish national territory in Birobidjan in the Far East on the banks of the Amur river.[10] Such a settlement would have had strategic significance in the troubled border region with Manchuria, especially after the Japanese conquest of that province in 1931. For about twenty years, even after World War II, attempts were made to reactivate the scheme, but it was finally abandoned. There are apparently not more than about 10,000 Jews in Birobidjan today, and a weekly Yiddish paper which appears there is flown in from Moscow.

One may view the Soviet efforts in the Crimea and in Birobidjan as yet further attempts at a territorialist solution, but it is difficult to place them in the context of Jewish attempts to escape political powerlessness. Other territorialist proposals were made or adopted by Jews. This was not the case in Russia, where the proposals seem to have originated largely from among the liberal non-Jewish cadres in the Party who would later be liquidated by Stalin as Rightist deviationists.

In the case of the Crimea, the 'Joint' (The American Jewish Joint Distribution Committee) was a full partner in the settlement attempts, but Jewish communists were by and large not sympathetic. The JDC was motivated by a desire to find an economically and politically secure position for the Russian Jews, and fairly large numbers of Russian Jews responded to its call. In the late twenties and early thirties many tried to improve their economic position through JDC-subsidized land settlement. But the same factors that militated against territorialist solutions elsewhere operated in Russia as well. In the course of the thirties, the Crimean settlement began to disintegrate because there were no emotional or national attachments to the 'Jewish' areas to compensate for the attraction of newly developing industries in the larger cities. Jews left the settlements in large numbers, and the project collapsed. The same is true for Birobidjan, where no outside factor such as the JDC operated.

Parenthetically, one might note the contradiction in the communist approach to the Jewish problem. On the one hand, Jewish national character was defined as a disappearing phenomenon, and its attempted revival as reactionary. On the other hand, Jewish communists tried to preserve Jewish culture within the framework of the communist regime, while the Party, its increasingly violent opposition to Zionism notwithstanding, accepted the basic Zionist tenet – i.e., the existence of a Jewish national entity – and proposed a territorial solution that would be in accordance with Soviet strategic interests.

The last non-Zionist attempt to attain a measure of political security and political power for the Jews to be discussed here was perhaps also the most important – that of the Bund. Its program has already been briefly outlined in the discussion of Soviet communism and Jewish nationalism. The Bund in Russia was dissolved, together with other independent expressions of Jewish aspirations, after the Bolshevik revolution. It became, however, very influential among the Jewish masses in the other eastern European Jewish centres, especially in Poland, where it drifted towards social democracy and tried to establish friendly liaisons with the Polish socialists. Between the two wars, the Bund fought for a socialist Polish republic in which Jewish workers would enjoy autonomy in the expression of their popular Yiddish culture. Despite partial successes in its attempts to create a united front with the Polish socialists, the Bund was ultimately forced to establish exclusively Jewish workers' organizations. These included self-defence groups to oppose the growing antisemitic attacks by Polish nationalists. The Polish socialists remained ambivalent: they could not establish close contacts with the Bund for fear of forfeiting the allegiance of large sections of the population infected with the antisemitic virus.

The Bund found itself struggling for the strengthening of the Jewish position, for Jewish defence against antisemitism, and for a place in the political power structure in eastern Europe. By implication, it denied the existence of a worldwide Jewish national entity embracing the Yiddish-speaking masses of eastern Europe and their descendants in the New World on the one hand and the Sephardi and Oriental Jews on the other hand. Jews, it believed, would have to find their permanent homes in their countries of birth, and seek a solution to the problems of security and cultural autonomy in each such country by joining with non-Jews in a struggle for an egalitarian society. The Bund therefore opposed Zionism as a utopian, escapist solution which diverted the Jewish masses from that progress and socialism which would ultimately solve the Jewish problem in its wake.

The failure of the Bund was poignantly underscored during the Holocaust by the discussions preceding the establishment of the Jewish Fighting Organization (ZOB) in the Warsaw ghetto in July-October 1942. Mauricy Orzech, the leader of the Bund, said that his organization would not join any specifically Jewish fighting force because it believed in the fighting unity of the Polish and Jewish masses against fascism: it would therefore wait for the Polish socialists to give the signal for the beginning of the struggle. The Bund would not join a nationalist Jewish resistance group (which, by the way, included the Jewish communists along with Zionists). It was not until October 1942, when all hope of intervention by the Polish underground had faded completely and the mass murder of the bulk of the Jewish population of Warsaw had already taken place against the background of complete Polish indifference, that the Bund decided to join in the establishment of the ZOB. The Bund thus finally joined the lonely Jewish fight against national extinction when only 60,000 out of the original 400,000 Warsaw Jews were still alive.[11]

The Zionists opposed the idea that the Jews were a religious group only; nor did they accept the notion, later developed by Stalin, that they were an inevitably disappearing nationality. Even Zionist socialists did not put unlimited faith in millenary socialist solutions. Nor, finally, did they accept the notion that Jews would immigrate *en masse* to a territory with which they had no historical, cultural, or emotional connection.

The Zionist movement, from its inception and during its development early in the present century, did encompass divergent trends: a religious wing which insisted on Jewish religion as the one legitimate expression of Jewish national feeling, and also a socialist wing which, in various degrees, believed in a worldwide socialist evolution or revolution that would ultimately guarantee the existence of the Jewish nation in its homeland. Herzl's territorialist notions regarding Uganda have already been mentioned. Still, despite its factionalism, Zionism slowly developed into the chief expression of Jewish national endeavour in the course of struggles, by no means always successful, against the other movements in Jewish life.

Zionism's fundamental notions were twofold: that the Jewish people all over the world are part of one national or ethnic entity, although they may continue to be perfectly loyal citizens in their respective countries; and that increasingly large numbers of Jews would, given the opportunity, concentrate in a specifically Jewish national centre in the Land of Israel, which would become a base for relative political power as well as a centre for the development of Jewish national culture. Based on such premises, Zionism can be seen as a national movement trying to extricate the Jewish people from a situation of political powerlessness which might leave them entirely defenceless in a world in which political clout was an important factor.[12]

Reacting to the external pressure which tended to isolate the Jew; postulating the futility of Jewish attempts to merge with European society; drawing on the age-old longing of Jews for an autonomous existence in their ancient homeland and on the strong religious and ethnic cohesion among Jews of eastern Europe; and, finally, attracting Jewish support with the revival of Hebrew culture and the prospects of social experiment, Zionism gradually emerged as the major political force among the Jewish people. It developed two parallel political aims: to protect the rights of the Jews in their countries of residence, and to further the cause of Jewish national aspiration in Palestine. This, indeed, was a radical departure in Jewish history.

II

How did Zionism try to gain support from uncommitted sections of Jewish communities in different countries? What was its underlying relationship to Great Britain, the holder of the Mandate over Palestine? Above all, how was the Zionist movement affected by the emerging threat of the Hitler regime? In the face of such problems, how did the Zionist movement continue its quest for relative political power for the Jewish people?

While we shall concentrate on the twenties and the thirties, it may be worth our while to survey very briefly the period preceding them. This period culminated in the Balfour Declaration of 1917, which promised the establishment of a Jewish 'National Home' in Palestine.

The foreign policy of the early Zionist movement was aimed at securing a charter for Jewish settlement from the imperial administrators of Palestine, the Turks. Palestine's Arab population early in the nineteenth century numbered about 300,000, and while their existence was not overlooked by Zionism, it was assumed that with large numbers of Jewish immigrants the Arabs would be reduced to a minority.[13] The Turks were approached, and the services of the great Powers were sought to influence Turkey to grant a charter. Herzl was especially eager to obtain the services of Britain for this purpose, a strategy which, in retrospect, appears very sensible. It certainly was similar to the policies of other incipient national movements in the nineteenth century, such as the Italian or Czech, for instance. British influence was all the more urgent because the Jews had nothing very impressive to offer in return for the charter.

In his memorandum to the Sultan, Herzl nevertheless extolled the benefits of modernization that Jewish settlement would bring, not only to Palestine but to the whole Ottoman Empire. In addition, he promised, Jewish funds would help to develop Ottoman industry and trade. Herzl did not grasp that in the eyes of many Turkish politicians these were arguments *against* the granting of a charter. An influx of Jewish capital which would control Turkish industry was the last thing the Turks wanted. Prior to World War I, then, Zionist goals in Palestine were frustrated. Jewish political power in the Diaspora was insufficient to exert the necessary pressure on the governments concerned. Besides, as we have seen, the Zionists were still a small minority among the Jews themselves.

Herzl had directed the attention of the Zionist movement to a very essential point. Like most small nations, the Jews needed a protector; as an alternative, they would have to exploit the disagreements of the great Powers to their advantage. Diaspora Jewry did exploit precisely this kind of political advantage during World War I, and in this period the Zionist movement also found its protector. During the war the Jews enjoyed a real choice: both the Central Powers and the Allies competed for their loyalties. Except for Czarist Russia, none of the Powers was anti-Zionist or overtly anti-Jewish. Indeed, as has recently been shown,[14] one of the main considerations which stirred the British to produce the Balfour Declaration was their fear that the Germans would make the Jews a similar promise; the official seat of the Zionist Organization was Germany, and the Germans did in fact produce their own declaration after the British had published theirs.

Another factor considered by the British Foreign Office was the presumed influence of Jews on political life both in the United States and – believe it or not – in Russia. In the U.S., the British hoped, Jews could be persuaded to abandon support for Germany (Jewish leadership in the U.S. was of German origin) and make a sizable contribution to the American war effort. In Russia, where Zionist influence was tremendously exaggerated in the minds of Foreign Office officials, a pro-Zionist policy might wean Jews away from communism and persuade them to favour the prosecution of the war against Germany. It appears that antisemitic tendencies underlay such bloated notions of Jewish power. A hostile version of similar notions had produced in Russia the 'Protocols of the Elders of Zion,' a forgery by the Czarist police which, it will be remembered, accused the Jews of trying to rule the world. In Britain, the belief in a world Jewish power led to an exaggerated view of Jewish influence and to a decision to prefer the Jews as allies. But the British also struck a note of realism: they adopted the outlines of an imperial scheme, originated by Sir Mark Sykes of the Foreign Office, which proposed that Britain's power in the Middle East should rest on an alliance with the three great national movements of the area: the Arab, the Jewish, and the Armenian.[15]

The Balfour Declaration was therefore the result, in a large measure, of the imagined power of the Jews. Little wonder that this Jewish power position disappeared at the war's end. American Jewry lost its clout in the Palestine question as a result of American government withdrawal from overseas affairs and also because of the disintegration of the inter-Jewish alliance, Zionist and non-Zionist, which had been forged in the United States toward the end of the war. Russian Jewry was isolated as the result of the Bolshevik Revolution. The emergent nationalist regimes in central and southeastern Europe slowly did away with the political and economic equality of Jews which had been written into their constitutions as a result of international pressure, largely at Jewish insistence.

In Palestine, the Zionists failed to exploit fully the opportunity inherent in the terms of the Mandate – a 'National Home' for the Jews which would not compromise the civil and religious rights of Arabs. The Russian Revolution had blocked the way to Palestine of Russian Jews. Others still hesitated to come. The Jewish world was not yet Zionist; Jews were not prepared to devote large resources to the construction of a Jewish society in Palestine, nor did they devise organizational instruments to implement large-scale plans.

The Zionist struggle for a limited power base for the Jewish people, moreover, had to meet opposition in Palestine, from the Arabs themselves and from an increasingly pro-Arab British administration. It was difficult to sustain support for Jewish national aspirations in the light of growing Arab strength, economic and political. The opposition of Palestine Arabs, and later of Arab nationalists generally, to Zionist settlement was by no means unknown either to the Jews or to the British, and the opposition grew. So did the Arab population. Under the British Mandate in the twenties and thirties, Zionist know-how and capital raised the standard of living to such a degree that Palestine attracted an unprecedented influx of Arabs, paralleling the more organized immigration of Jews.

In Zionist eyes, the Arabs were members of a nation that was attaining independence in vast areas, rich in natural resources. There seemed no reason why they should object to three to four per cent of their number becoming a minority in the historic national home of the hitherto homeless Jews. After all, Jews had been a minority everywhere for the whole period of their Diaspora. Why could *some* Arabs not be a minority in a Jewish country? When in 1937 the Royal Commission on Palestine (the Peel Commission) declared that the struggle in Palestine was one of right against right, the Zionists replied that the right of the Arabs was relative: their nation had a vast homeland, occupying a not inconsiderable part of the globe. The right of the Jews was absolute; they had nowhere else to go. In 1937, moreover, this claim was more than rhetorical. As the Nazi threat grew, the Western democracies closed their doors.

In its struggle for a national power base, Zionism insisted that it wanted to avoid injuring or displacing the Arab population of Palestine. Lands were acquired by purchase, and tenants were compensated even when they had no legal title to the land that was sold by absentee landowners. A British attempt in 1929 to show that Arabs were being dispossessed by Jews elicited claims by only 3,271 tenants, of whom 664 were vindicated by largely sympathetic courts. Even if, as some claimed, Arab tenants were suspicious of British intentions and did not therefore register all their titles to land, it is hardly likely that the number of claims would have been substantially larger without such suspicions.[16]

There is curious naiveté coursing through the discussions of Zionist leaders up to the thirties. The Zionists tended to see the problem of Arab opposition in political-economic terms. As the standard of living of the Arab population rose, it was believed, objections to Jewish immigration would diminish. Arab immigration into Palestine of Syrians (Hauranis), Egyptians, Sudanese, and Bedouins seemed to prove that the Zionist project was beneficial to the Arab people. This was a serious miscalculation; a full belly proved no substitute for political independence. Besides, Jewish capital was invested for Jewish national purposes; Arabs benefited from it only indirectly through the general rise in living standards, and not through any direct investment for Arab development.

Politically, Zionists demanded only Jewish self-government in Palestine. It was Arab hostility that gradually united the majority of factions behind the demand for an independent Jewish state. Chaim Weizmann had declared in 1931 against the idea of a Jewish state, and David Ben-Gurion did the same in his evidence before the Peel Commission in 1937 (although he subsequently supported the Peel Report's recommendation for the partition of Palestine). Both leaders originally supported a federative solution whereby political power would be shared on a basis of parity without regard to the actual majority in the country. The left-wing group of Hashomer Hatsair supported this solution until the summer of 1947.

All Zionist groups, however, except for the small group of intellectuals around Judah L. Magnes and Martin Buber, advocated free Jewish immigration to achieve a Jewish majority in Palestine, in the belief that no power base would otherwise be possible. (The Magnes-Buber group advocated Jewish immigration up to half the population). It was precisely over this question of immigration that all attempts to arrive at a peaceful solution with the Arabs collapsed. The Arabs of Palestine already constituted the majority living on the land and would ultimately establish their right to independence, or so they presumed. They did not see why they should give up this potential advantage.

It was only gradually that the central importance of the Jewish-Arab struggle in Palestine, the Land of Israel, dawned on the Zionist leadership. Well into World War II, leading Zionists believed that the way to solve the Jewish-Arab quarrel would be to have the Great Powers, preferably Britain, impose a compromise solution which would grant the Jews most of what they wanted (political autonomy, free immigration) and mollify the Arabs by creating a semi-independent Arab Federation of which Jewish Palestine might become a part.[17]

The Labour wing in Zionism, and also Dr Weizmann's moderate General Zionists, which together dominated the policies of the Zionist movement after 1933, saw in the Arab national movement in Palestine an essentially artificial creation of the British. The Zionists tended to accuse the British in Palestine of a policy of 'divide and rule,' and turned to the British in London to correct such Machiavellian excesses. It is of course quite true that the British supported and encouraged the formation of Arab political groupings in Palestine. It is also true that these groups increasingly tended to follow the extreme nationalist and later expressly pro-fascist leadership of the Mufti of Jerusalem, Hajj Amin al-Husseini. It is equally true that most of the Palestinian Arab leadership was recruited from among the wealthiest and most patriarchally minded feudal-type landowners. But what escaped the attention of even perceptive Zionist leaders of the twenties and thirties was the fact that Palestine's Arab intelligentsia was groping for a genuine national expression of its own.

Attempts were made by Zionist leaders to gain Arab supporters for compromise plans. However, only one serious contender for Arab leadership, Fakhri Bey Nashashibi,[18] was prepared for serious talks on Arab-Jewish understanding based on recognition of Jewish as well as Arab rights, and he was ultimately murdered by henchmen of the pro-fascist Mufti in 1938. Behind-the-scenes discussions, with and without British mediation, took place at various times with Arab leaders, but they all turned out to be fruitless since the Arabs would not agree to the basic Jewish demand for immigration. These halfhearted attempts of Jewish leadership to pave the way for the establishment of a Jewish political power base by some mutually advantageous agreement with the Arabs – those of Palestine and, in 1939,[19] those of the then existing Arab states – were thus frustrated.

III

In this attempt to trace the emergence of the Jews from political powerlessness, we have ignored some related developments in the United States of America. We must now turn to the situation there, because America's Jewry played a vital role in the establishment of what finally became the State of Israel.

One tends to forget that a scant forty years ago there was, or appeared to be, a real danger that a very powerful antisemitic movement would arise in the United States. A series of public opinion polls conducted in the late thirties and early forties revealed a strong minority sentiment against Jews in general, and an overwhelming majority sentiment against the immigration to America of more Jews fleeing from Hitler.[20] Jewish political influence was small. Jews voted overwhelmingly Democrat, and identified largely with the liberal elements in the country. Conservative politicians, apart from their anti-Jewish prejudices, had no great incentive to woo the Jews from the opposite camp. As for President Roosevelt, the Jews had no choice but to support him: he, and the liberals voting for him, appeared to be the main barrier to the rise of antisemitism in the United States.

There was also a tendency in American society to see America as a melting-pot rather than a multi-ethnic society. Jews, like others, lived in a climate there that encouraged a radical break with ethnic or even with religious traditions that were not part of the American Christian mainstream.

Jewish leaders in the U.S. were, until well into the thirties, individuals of German-Jewish ancestry such as Jacob H. Schiff, Louis Marshall, Cyrus Adler, and Felix M. Warburg. They demonstrated a preference for quiet diplomacy to achieve political ends, whether intervention in favour of threatened Jewish groups abroad or struggle against American antisemitism. It was widely assumed that Jews in America had no real power, but they may have had some influence owing to their identification with the leaders of American liberalism and also to the relatively large number of American Jewish intellectuals who rose to prominence in various branches of the government. The effectiveness of the Jewish leadership's quiet diplomacy cannot be denied at least up to a point. American intervention in favour of Rumanian Jews in the latter half of the last century, American responses to the Jewish plight in Czarist Russia, and even the positive attitude of the U.S. government to demands for Jewish minority rights in eastern Europe after World War I can all be ascribed to it.

Jewish political *power*, however, was indeed paltry, and in the liberal world toward which the great Republic was presumably progressing, ethnic or nationalistic power was expected to become superfluous, a deplorable remnant of a past age.[21] The small Zionist movement in America at first fitted well into this general scheme of things. American Jews were Americans first and foremost; but they belonged to an ancient culture and would support the establishment of a national home in Palestine for their less fortunate co-religionists who were denied the blessings of American equality.

Jewish pressure groups thus took quite some time to develop in America. One can perhaps see in the establishment of the American Jewish Congress toward the end of World War I an early sign of things to come. But the first clear attempts to work for specifically Jewish interests were initiated only in the thirties. The anti-Nazi Boycott Movement, headed by Samuel Untermayer (a member of the German-Jewish 'aristocracy') and supported by large numbers of Jews of east European background, tried to enlist Jewish and non-Jewish public opinion for an economic struggle against Germany. It failed to bring Germany to its knees, but it helped to create an anti-Nazi public opinion which would support Roosevelt's increasingly anti-Hitler stand.

The anti-German boycott movement, and other manifestations of American Jewish muscle in the thirties, did not turn the Jews into a substantial political force. A good case in point is the conference on refugees convened by Roosevelt at Evian in July 1938 to which I have already referred.[22] The conference was intended to take the wind out of the liberal demand to help the

Jews while keeping the restrictionists happy by promising a tight lid on immigration quotas and on any financing of the Jewish flight from Germany. This philanthropic attitude fell short of needs in the hour of the great Jewish tragedy. During the war itself, the Jews were politically impotent. They could not do anything that might be interpreted as anti-Roosevelt action; after all, Roosevelt fought the anti-Hitler war. The most important pro-Jewish American action of the war was the establishment, in January 1944, of the War Refugee Board, whose task, we have seen, was to bring help to persecuted minorities in Europe, primarily Jews, through unconventional means if necessary. The WRB certainly made some difference in American policy towards the Jews under Nazi rule; but by the time it came into existence most of the mass murder had already taken place.

The WRB was established largely at the initiative of a few young non-Jewish officials in the Treasury, which was headed by a Jew, Henry Morgenthau. It appears, in fact, that Morgenthau was driven to intervene with Roosevelt by his energetic subordinates and did not originate the move himself.[23] While we can only guess at the reasons that induced Roosevelt to accept the idea of the WRB, however, we cannot ignore the increasing political power at this point of Jews.

Where and how did this political power begin to grow? A great deal more research is still needed into this vital topic.[24] What appears clear today is that major strides were taken during the war, and that the Zionist movement in its various manifestations – the Zionist Organization of America, the American Jewish Congress, the Emergency Committee to Save the Jewish People, and others – were the prime movers. Notwithstanding their factional disputes, organizations such as those of the Revisionists (e.g., the Jewish Army committee founded by Peter Bergson, which in 1943 became the Emergency Committee), and the Zionist Emergency Committee (after 1943, Council) led by Rabbis Stephen S. Wise and Abba Hillel Silver, not only began organizing typically American 'grass roots' pressure groups, but also managed to form non-Jewish bodies in support of Jewish demands. These groups, demanding Jewish participation in the war in Jewish Army units, the rescue of Jews from Nazi Europe, and the establishment of Palestine as a Jewish Commonwealth, formed the basis upon which Jewish power was to be built in the years after the war.

While we are on the subject of postwar Jewish power, two caveats. One: although the first attempts at creating a mass basis for a Jewish political power were made by Silver during the war, the Zionist movement still had a long way to go. Its influence was often sporadic and, especially in 1946 and 1947, it was less effective than pro-Jewish gentile public opinion in the United

States. Two: the Jewish vote began to be an effective instrument only in the later stages of World War II and beyond. This was due to the relatively slow rise of a native-born American Jewish population which could employ its acquired American political instincts. With the rise of this new generation, the Jewish vote became important – no American politician cared to find out whether such a vote really existed or not; he assumed it did, and reacted accordingly.

Jewish influence alone was very limited, however, even when the Jewish vote was taken into account. What appears to have been decisive was the readiness of the non-Jewish American public to support some basic Jewish aspirations. This may be surprising when one considers how widespread anti-Jewish attitudes had been only a few years prior to the rise of pro-Zionist sentiment in America. For such a drastic change to have been feasible, there must have been elements in American backgrounds and cultural attitudes that were susceptible to pro-Jewish influence. We may well look for these backgrounds in the traditions of American Christianity, which regarded the Holy Land, the Hebrew language, and the Zion-centered Jewish aspirations as part and parcel an eschatology accepted by many Americans.[25] (Such a background does not necessarily contradict variants of anti-Jewish sentiment; support for a Jewish national existence might mean that Jews belong to their national home rather than to their countries of adoption.) Beyond this, American public opinion was dramatically affected by the impact of the Nazi horrors as seen through the eyes of American soldiers who liberated the concentration camps of West Germany. The basic decency of the American people was outraged by these reports, and the immediate reaction was to try to compensate at least the survivors by letting them go where they wanted. The long-term reaction to the discovery of the camps was a growing feeling of guilt in the democratic world that had allowed these horrors to happen. Finally, Silver's 'grass roots' organization fitted into the accepted patterns of American political life. It developed a 'pressure group' which in the American system was recognized as a legitimate body of American citizens trying to influence their government's policies on matters that concerned them. The impact of the Holocaust thus was the primary factor propelling American Jewry into the exercise of political power as a legitimate part of the American political system. The aim of the Jews' political struggle was the establishment of Jewish political autonomy in the land of Israel. Incidentally, this also meant the rise of American Jewish political power.

IV

The story of the Jewish emergence from powerlessness turned on the securing of a Jewish state. The setting up of Israel, and the parallel rise of Jewish political power in the United States, created new challenges and new difficulties, but few Jews would trade them for the old ones.

From 1945 to 1948, the consequences of the Holocaust were decisive in the struggle to establish Israel. It is this period which we shall now consider. One must caution at the outset, however, that our access to the original sources is still restricted, and those documents which are available go no further than 1947.[26]

The Biltmore Resolution of May 1942, of the Zionist movement in the U.S., demanded that Palestine become a Jewish Commonwealth as part of a Mid-Eastern Federation or as part of the British Empire. The resolution was based on the assumption that after World War II Europe would contain millions of Jewish refugees for whom the most natural solution would be immigration to Palestine. Even when the dimensions of the destruction of European Jewry became known in the summer of 1942, this resolution was not amended. It was ratified in Jerusalem in November 1942, after the annihilation of European Jews, who formed the basis for its demand, was common knowledge. But it is probably true that the shock attending the news of the mass murder was too great to be immediately translated into political action. On the other hand, the discussions following the November meeting in Jerusalem show that the response of the Zionists was to demand their independent state from the democratic world with even greater fervour.[27]

The news from Europe caused widespread paralysis and despair. The general assumption, especially in Palestine, was that nothing could be done, that European Jewry was lost and there was no way in which the weak, numerically small (500,000) and uninfluential Yishuv could help their surviving brothers from such a distance. The rescue operations which were initiated were undertaken out of a sense of hopelessness.[28]

Nevertheless, Jews, especially in Palestine, came to see the Biltmore Resolution as a symbol of the Jewish will to live as a community. Tremendous enthusiasm arose for the demand for a Jewish State, and increased as the war drew to its close. The main argument now was that the few surviving remnants would be unable to return to their former homes. It was also deeply felt that the world 'owed' the Jews a political sanctuary in the form of a state.

This was not the view of the British government. Faced with a choice between the Arabs, who would soon control the world's richest oil resources and whose support was essential if Britain was to maintain its hold over the strategic routes through the Middle East, and the powerless Jews, the British had published their White Paper of May 1939. They had come down on the side of the Arabs – a Palestine State with a permanent Arab majority would be set up in ten years' time, and Jewish immigration stopped after permitting another 75,000 Jews to enter Palestine; land acquisition by Jews in ninety-five per cent of the country would cease. In this White Paper the Jewish claim to a developing, growing autonomous polity had been rejected.

On 16 October 1944, the Jewish Agency submitted a memorandum to the Mandate authorities which stated that, of the six million Jews in prewar Europe outside Britain and Russia, no more than 1,500,000 remained alive, and even those had not yet been saved. In addition, the number of Jews in the Soviet Union had been reduced by one million. The root of this tragedy, it was argued, was the Jews' lack of a national home. So long as this remained the case, solutions such as Hitler's would remain tempting to demagogues and tyrants. Morally speaking, moreover, it was not realistic to offer the remnants of European Jewry a return to the *status quo ante* sweetened with mere philanthropy and paper promises.

A second Jewish Agency memorandum presented on 22 May 1945, just two weeks after the end of the war, emphasized this point again. During the period between these two communications, Lord Moyne, who incidentally was one of the supporters of the plan to partition Palestine and set up a Jewish state, was murdered in Cairo by Jews of the 'Stern Group' from Palestine. The murder ended whatever chances existed for Churchill and other pro-Zionist Conservatives to intervene in favour of partition. The 1939 White Paper remained in effect until the Labour Party took over the government.

As the cessation of hostilities had drawn near, the full dimensions of the disaster in Europe were revealed to the Jewish people. The first organized reactions came from the Diaspora by the end of 1944. The remnants of the Jewish ghettos, the forest fighters, and the Polish Jews who first returned from their places of refuge in the Soviet Union debated three possible courses of action. The first was to take the Jewish survivors out of eastern Europe as quickly as possible and bring them to shores from which they could reach Palestine. The second emphasized the need to take revenge on a large scale against the perpetrators of the Holocaust. The third called for an orderly exodus – legal or illegal – from eastern Europe, with some of the leaders of the fighting youth movements staying behind to organize the Jewish remnants and stay with them as long as they remained there.

Plans for revenge were tried, and they failed. But those who determined to bring about the mass exodus of Holocaust survivors from eastern Europe were more successful. They organized the *Brichah*,[29] and sought out Palestinian *shlichim* (emissaries) in Rumania, and later in Italy, with whom the escape could be plotted. We shall have more to say about the Brichah presently.

To digress for a moment, it should be emphasized that it was the survivors of the Holocaust who found their way to Eretz-Yisrael through the Palestinian *shlichim* in Europe; it was not the *shlichim* who initiated the contact. The failure of Zionist Palestine to reach these remnants was to have important emotional, conceptual, and social implications in the years to come. It led to a repression of this vast movement's history in the Israeli national consciousness. Armed action against the British in Palestine was (and is) extolled at the expense of the story of the Holocaust survivors.

This repression of the story of the Brichah was, of course, not decided consciously; it was natural for Israelis to try to make the struggle for Israel the work, mainly or solely, of Israeli youth. But the fact that very little, if anything, is taught in Israeli schools about the Holocaust survivors' Odyssey to their ancestral land distorts the collective memory of Israeli society. Revealingly, the 'illegal immigration' (Aliyah Bet) on ships to Palestine is the only part of the mass move which is depicted. This is so because on the ships the survivors were only passive participants, while the planning, organization, and execution of the transports were the responsibility of the Yishuv's underground. But in the mass exodus from eastern Europe, the first *shlichim* from Jewish Palestine reached Poland only in October 1945, about ten months after the organization of the Brichah and the beginning of the movement out of Poland into Rumania.

The eastern European Holocaust survivors were, by that time, a fairly homogeneous and united group with a more or less accepted leadership consisting of fighters and partisans, most of whom had been members of the Zionist youth movements before the war. In their meetings with the representatives of Eretz-Yisrael, these leaders expressed their fundamental beliefs: antisemitism had not disappeared with the defeat of Germany; the Holocaust would repeat itself in the future; and finally, the Jewish people had to prepare for such an eventuality by readying the Diaspora for defence and response, and by readying Palestine as a haven and fortress. Abba Kovner, for example, the former commander of the Vilna ghetto rebels, expressed these thoughts in a speech to the Jewish Brigade (a Palestinian Jewish unit in the British Army) on 17 July 1945: 'But what are we to do if in our sick souls – or are they healed already? – we bear not only the vision of the past, but also that of the future. And we feel with all our senses the breath of the approaching slaughtering knife. The knife which lies in ambush in every corner, on every path and highway of Europe. The new knife was born on the fields of Maidanek, Ponar, and Treblinka where millions of the masses of tens of nations saw how it was done – so easily, so simply, so quietly.'[30] From this he drew the conclusion that Palestine, Jewish Palestine, must know how to save the remnants of this people: the Holocaust survivors would bring a warning which was beyond existing ideological debate and party bickering. For Kovner, it had been 'the sense of falling,' the powerlessness of the Jewish masses, that was the most disastrous aspect of the Holocaust experience.

These and similar sentiments found expression in early 1945 in newly formed Jewish organizations which sought to break the party framework of the Zionist movement in the name of the Holocaust's bitter lesson. Thus, an organization of east European survivors was founded in Rumania in April 1945, and the United Zionist Federation was established in the DP camps in Germany after the war. All these movements, significantly, disappeared or changed radically after a short time. It turned out that when the survivors met with practical problems of a living Zionist movement represented by parties whose support came from people living under the more or less normal conditions of the Yishuv, Jewish life in that normal society was stronger than the political and organizational expression given to the new message of destruction.

Still, the events which took place in Poland after the liberation seemed to confirm the morbid prognosis of the spokesmen of the Holocaust remnants. Only 80,000 Jews were left in Poland in the summer of 1945 and 175,000 were to return from Asiatic Russia in 1946 under the terms of a new treaty. The Jews of eastern Europe – Poland, Lithuania, western Russia, and even Slovakia and parts of Rumania and Hungary – found themselves in a very difficult situation. There had been widespread antisemitism in these countries before the war, and the Nazi murder machine had shown the local population how easily all moral impediments to the annihilation of their Jewish neighbours could be swept away. Hatred of Jews did not therefore diminish, but on the contrary increased. Those who suffered from feelings of guilt at having participated in the murder of Jews wanted to do away with the few witnesses that survived. Others, who had only stolen or taken the property of the Jews, were understandably eager not to have the claimants return. As a result, many Jews found life in their old homes impossible.

In addition to all of this, the Polish Jews who did return to their former homes soon became caught up in the struggle between the communist minority that had gained power with Soviet help, and the great majority of the population which did not want such a regime imposed on them. Civil wars broke out in Poland and in the western Ukraine in which the Jews were identified with the communists. The majority of the regime's opponents came from rightist and centrist groups which had been antisemitic before the war and now found it easy to return to prewar slogans equating the Jews with the communists.

The Jews were a numerically small group, virtually unprotected (the nascent governments were still incapable of protecting them), and were forced to support the new regime as the only power which might be able to save them. For their part, the new governments in Poland and in other 'people's democracies,' and the Soviet authorities in the western parts of Russia, all viewed the Jews, grudgingly, as one of the few loyal pillars upon which to build their new order. This accounted for the relatively large numbers of Jews in the administrations of these governments, a fact that reinforced the identification of the Jews with the new regimes.

But the impotence of the new Polish leftist regime was underscored by the high number of Jews murdered during its first three years. Jews were often thrown off trains, or left to the mercy of the murderous antisemitic underground. Jews who returned to towns and hamlets which were outside the government's reach were murdered upon arrival. Even in the large cities, there were occasional pogroms in which Jews were slain. According to Polish government statistics, 351 Jews were murdered between November 1944 and October 1945; many others were attacked, robbed and wounded. Anti-Jewish riots took place in Cracow on 20 August 1945, in Sosnowiec on 25 October, in Lublin on November 19. These riots reached epidemic proportions in 1946, the very time when the Jews who had fled to Soviet Asia were returning to Poland. The murderous activity reached its peak in the pogrom at Kielce on 4 July 1946, in which 42 Jews were brutally murdered after having been accused of using Christian blood for ceremonial purposes. The Kielce pogrom had an enormous effect on the Jewish remnants in Poland, and this was most understandable. Right in the heart of Poland, a district city of 60,000 inhabitants which was also the seat of the local bishop, and only one year after Hitler's defeat, a pogrom incited by a blood-libel took place – a pogrom, one must add, in which the local government militia, members of the clergy, and even a socialist factory director and his workers took part.

The events of July 1946 led to a panic, in the course of which 100,000 bewildered Jews left Poland and the surrounding countries within three months. The stream of Jewish refugees flowed irregularly to the south in 1946, and later to the west. It was led by the Brichah and continued under the leadership of the Mossad (organization for illegal immigration to Palestine) and its emissaries.

This was the high point of the Brichah's activities. We ought now to know more about it. Founded by Abba Kovner, the Brichah was at first led mainly by ex-partisans and returnees from Soviet central Asia. It organized frontier crossings, and forged papers – mainly Red Cross documents purporting to be permits for repatriation which enabled their holders to move to their 'homes' in the countries which they wanted to enter. It was financed largely by the JDC – unwittingly so, because the JDC supplied food and clothing to the 'transients,' and thus enabled them to carry on with their journeys. In early 1946 a coordinating secretariat of the Brichah was established in Czechoslovakia, headed by a Palestinian emissary, Levi Argov. By the summer of that year, area commands were established, liaison with the Paris centre of the Mossad was functioning, and Jewish refugees and Brichah activists could be moved from Poland to Italy or France or Germany, equipped with suitable documents – or by arrangement with border guards. There was no hard-and-fast hierarchy; an overwhelming sense of purpose made this remarkable mass movement function.[31]

The Brichah was Europe's largest organized illegal migration in this century. More than a quarter of a million Jews moved out of eastern Europe, the majority coming from Poland and the others from Lithuania, Rumania, Hungary, Slovakia, and Yugoslavia. At first, in the summer of 1945, they went to Italy with the hope of getting from there to Palestine as quickly as possible. But the roads were soon blocked, and the Italian DP camps filled. The number of illegal immigrants smuggled into Palestine declined. Italy remained saturated so another place had to be found for the refugees.

Germany and Austria were then suggested. The first to move in this direction was the Brichah leadership in Poland, which saw the American Zone of occupation as the only place where the Jewish survivors could get the appropriate physical care. It is probable that by this time (August 1945), one motive behind such reasoning was to create a political fact by concentrating the refugees in one place. The Palestinian regiments in the British Army reached a similar conclusion, and they too began to direct people to Germany.

David Ben-Gurion also pushed for this solution. He visited Germany in October 1945 and met with Generals Eisenhower and Bedell Smith. In a memorandum submitted after a visit to Jewish camps he made several demands, the decisive one being that Jews from eastern Europe be allowed to enter American zones of occupation and be granted the status of displaced persons. The generals agreed, for reasons I shall elaborate below. Ben-Gurion's intentions were clearly expressed in his report of 21 November to the Jewish Agency. 'If we succeed in concentrating a quarter million Jews in the American zone, it will increase the American pressure [on the British]. Not because of the financial aspects of the problem – that does not matter to them – but because they see no future for these people outside Eretz-Yisrael.'[32]

The Zionist leadership feared that a large proportion of the many tens of thousands of Jews concentrated in the displaced persons camps in Germany and Austria would seek a way of reaching countries overseas rather than waiting until the gates of Palestine would be opened to them. There was some basis for such apprehensions; many Jewish survivors were anxious to pick up the threads of their lives. And if thousands of Jews did indeed go to the West, this would seriously endanger the struggle of the Jews for their state. The nucleus of those determined to reach Palestine was large, but the Jews brought to the camps by this nucleus had suffered so much; if the rich Western countries had been willing to accept them, it is probable that many would have gone.

Such was the opinion of many of the people on the spot, like the Palestinian emissary, Chaim Yahil, who headed the relief groups sent from Palestine to the DP camps in November 1945. It was also the opinion of an American Jew, Major Irving Heymont, who claimed at the end of 1947 that 'the establishment of a Jewish state did not noticeably influence the "Drang nach Amerika".'[33] It is likely, in fact, that if the DP population had been given equal opportunities to go to Palestine or to America, half of them would have joined Diaspora Jewry in America. This was true after the UN decision of November 1947, and it was certainly true of the year 1945-6 when the Jewish state seemed like a distant dream.

Practically speaking, however, America was still closed. True, President Truman had issued a directive to the U.S. immigration authorities in December 1945 giving first priority to the people in the displaced persons camps in Germany. But Jews were not the only displaced persons in German camps. In August 1945, after large numbers of Jewish concentration camp survivors had returned to countries such as France, Hungary, and Czechoslovakia, there were 50,000 Jews in the DP camps – before the quarter of a million Jews arrived from the east. But there were also 800,000 non-Jews, among them many Nazi collaborators of eastern European origin – murderers of Jews, former soldiers in the German army, and others of questionable background; but these people were mainly farmers or labourers and their employment prospects in America made them, ironically, appear more desirable to the American consuls who granted the visas than the Jewish tradesmen who had wasted away for years in the Nazi concentration camps or on the *kolkhozes* of Central Asia.

From 1945 to 1948, no more than 12,000 Jewish DP camp inmates entered the United States. Opportunities to emigrate to countries like England, South Africa, and Australia were no better. Assimilation among the Germans was not psychologically possible for the Jewish masses, and a return to the East was out of the question. Thus, the very situation Ben-Gurion had anticipated hopefully in November 1945 materialized. A pool of potential immigrants to Palestine was formed under American auspices.

The American military commanders were most eager to be rid of these Jews, inasmuch as a Jewish presence in Germany interfered with the increasingly pro-German policy of the American authorities. The only place they could be sent, if America would not accept them, was Palestine; and the way to achieve this goal was by pressuring Britain. For the Jews, the crucial political objective of the period was to press America to solve the problem of the Jewish Holocaust survivors, who were in DP camps under American supervision, but whose future lay in the hands of Whitehall.

At this point we must ask an important question. Why did the United States government agree to become entangled in the Palestine issue by admitting these Jews into the areas under its supervision in the fall of 1945, and again after the Kielce pogrom in the summer of 1946? The answer is very complex. We have many accounts of the tremendous impression that the discovery of the Nazi concentration camps made on the American officers and soldiers who liberated them. A mixture of deep shock and guilt seized them when they realized how little the free world had done to avert the Holocaust. Many officers now tended to support Jewish emigration from eastern Europe to a country the Jews wanted to build up as their own. On the other hand, evidence of an increasingly antisemitic attitude in the middle ranks in the U.S. Army also exists. But such attitudes, paradoxically perhaps, also tended to favour emigration to Palestine.

Those officers who opposed entry of Jews into the U.S. zones had to face a different problem: the only way the Jews could be prevented from entering American-occupied Germany was by the use of force. From a moral and political point of view, it was impossible in 1945 to order American soldiers to use arms against the Jewish victims of Hitlerism.

The final decision, however, was not taken primarily by the army, but at the highest political level. Earl G. Harrison, a Protestant law expert from Princeton, was went to Germany in June 1945 by the Intergovernmental Committee for Refugees. President Truman asked Harrison to check the situation in the Jewish camps while he was in Germany. The president's request came in the wake of a veritable flood of letters by Jewish chaplains and soldiers (and non-Jewish soldiers) in Germany to organizations and VIPs in the United States. The latter, in turn, turned to the White House with demands that steps be taken to alleviate the situation. Among these was Secretary of the Treasury Henry Morgenthau.

Truman was a new president who was unsure of his political strength. His honest humanitarian approach was never in doubt, and we know of his personal ties with Jews. There must have been additional motivations for him to send Harrison, but historians have still to determine the effects of Jewish and non-Jewish groups on American public opinion during this first stage. In any event, it is clear that Harrison's report to Truman in August 1945 was the beginning of gradually increasing American pressure on Britain. In the report, in which the facts were highly exaggerated, Harrison accused the American army, rather unfairly, of cruel and inhuman treatment of the Jewish survivors, and went so far as to compare American soldiers with the SS. The solution he suggested was the admission of 100,000 Jews to Palestine. Such an act would solve the problem of the 50,000 Jews then in the camps, and could take the sting out of Zionist demands regarding Polish Jewry as well.

The Harrison report brought about several crucial results. First of all it aroused the president's wrath against the army, and this finally resulted in the publication of the report in the press. Public opinion turned increasingly against the heads of the army. The latter, consequently, tried not to quarrel with the Jews, and determined not to interfere with their entry into the American zone. It was Harrison's report which was behind Eisenhower's and Bedell Smith's agreement to Ben-Gurion's demands in October. A further result was President Truman's effort to persuade the British to allow the immigration of 100,000 survivors to Palestine.

It would be distorting the truth to emphasize the efforts American Jews made to influence the president without taking into account the activities of non-Jews, although, again, there is a dearth of basic data in this important area. It is clear, however, that the Protestant and, to some extent, the Catholic communities in the United States – led by congressmen and senators from places where barely a single Jew resided (like Senator King of Utah) – contributed to a favourable climate of opinion regarding the immigration of Holocaust survivors to Palestine and the establishment of a Jewish state. It is important to ascertain the role played by Jewish organizations in general, and the Zionist Emergency Council under Abba Hillel Silver in particular, in convincing non-Jewish Americans to adopt this view. It is probable that direct Jewish influence was slight; but religious and political traditions, which viewed the immigration of Jews to Palestine as something natural and just, caused Americans to be particularly susceptible to Jewish political argument. At the same time, in part a Palestinian solution was seen as a way to prevent the Jews from entering the United States.

Responding to such pressures, American policy-makers set out two clear-cut political goals that held sway until August 1946. The first was to influence Britain to allow the entry of 100,000 Jewish immigrants into Palestine so that the Jews could be taken out of the DP camps in the American zones of Germany and Austria. The second was to make it clear to Britain that America did not want to be embroiled in the Palestinian question. She was not going to supply soldiers to enforce any political solution, and she was leaving Britain with the job of deciding Palestine's future. This second line of argument was motivated by internal American pressure not to expand the U.S. government's political and military obligations, and to leave the Middle East in the hands of the English ally. On 16 August 1945, President Truman expressed his interest in the entry of as many Jews as possible into Palestine as long as the matter could be settled through diplomatic channels, but he had no intention of sending half a million soldiers to maintain the peace there. (This number was based on an estimate of the U.S. War Department that Palestine's Jews would need the support of 400,000 additional soldiers to be able to face the Arabs.)

In August and September 1945 the new Labour government in Britain dealt intensively with the problem of Palestine. After the deliberation of a special committee, the government decided to continue the White Paper policy rather than follow pro-Zionist resolutions passed at the Labour Party convention; the latter were dismissed as merely 'suggestions' to the government. This decision, prompted by the Labour desire to win the support of Arab nationalists, and taken in the light of the increasing weakness of the British Empire as well as the government's decision to leave India, clashed with Truman's demand for the immigration of 100,000 Jews.

Britain was most anxious to get the United States to share the responsibility for Palestine and the Middle East in general, and therefore suggested the establishment of an Anglo-American Committee to solve the problem of the refugees. The United States was ready to accede to this request on condition that the future of the refugees be discussed along with the possibility of their absorption into Palestine. Once again the Americans stressed that their only interest in any deliberation on Palestine was as a place which could absorb the displaced Jews. In the complicated negotiations preceding the establishment of the committee, however, the Americans found it difficult to avoid deliberations about Palestine's future. In the end, the committee was empowered to deal with Jewish DPs in Europe and with the future political regime in Palestine. British Foreign Secretary Ernest Bevin privately promised the members of the committee that his government would implement any unanimous recommendations. The committee was set up in November 1945.

Any thesis which depicts two Western imperialisms – American and British – fighting for control of the Middle East is therefore quite false. Indeed, the opposite is true. Britain asked for American intervention in Palestine in an attempt to free herself of an insufferable yoke, while America tried hard not to let Britain impose any such responsibility upon her.

The British government hoped, of course, that the committee would find in favour of Britain's anti-Zionist policy. But the very reverse happened. The committee unanimously called for the admittance of 100,000 Jews into Palestine – in line with Truman's desires. Moreover, while its conclusions regarding the future of the country were vague, they were clearly in the spirit of suggestions calling for bi-national rule and continued Jewish immigration.

Contrary to Bevin's promise, Britain refused to implement the committee's findings. It has been said many times that the price Britain paid for her refusal to abide by the committee's main recommendation – to allow 100,000 immigrants into the country – was the loss of rule over Palestine. An immigration of such proportions would no doubt have dulled the edge of the Zionist claims, based mainly on the plight of the DPs. An immigration of 100,000 of the 150,000 Jewish refugees in the camps (before the Kielce pogrom of summer 1946) would also have put off the Jewish-British confrontation regarding the future of Palestine. Such an immigration would have strengthened the Yishuv internally, but Arab numerical superiority would have been easily maintained. The British refused to risk the entry of additional Jews, however, and were apparently determined to end the whole attempt to found a Jewish national home.

In the summer of 1946, matters reached a critical stage. When the British refused to carry out the recommendations of the Anglo-American Committee, a new Anglo-American 'expert' committee was appointed whose findings (in July 1946) backed British policy. The goal was to freeze the development of the Yishuv, and leave the country under a British regime whose policy was pro-Arab. In the United States there was a loud outcry against this new development and, under pressure from public opinion, President Truman announced that he did not support the British program. This happened early in August 1946, after the Kielce pogrom, when the consequent mass migration made the figure of 100,000 somewhat outdated. The president had wanted to stay away from Palestinian Jewish problems. But in August an initiative was launched by the Jewish Agency which suggested the partition of Palestine and prompted the United States to make a declaration in October which, mistakenly interpreted, seemed to favour partition as well. We shall return to this declaration.

First, I should like to clarify the influence the Yishuv, its underground movements, and its organization for illegal immigration, had on the processes that have been described. The Yishuv influenced the events in Europe directly in two main ways: through the Jewish Palestinian units in the British Army, and through the *shlichim* who worked in the Brichah and illegal immigration programs. The Jewish units, mainly the Jewish Brigade (which had seen some action against the Germans in the closing stages of the campaign in Italy), discovered Holocaust survivors in the liberated concentration camps of

Austria and south Germany in June 1945. Their influence on the survivors was tremendous – with their Jewish insignia they inspired confidence and self-assurance among people whom the Nazis had tried to dehumanize for years. Under the influence of the Palestinians and of rabbis who served as chaplains in the U.S. Army, the survivors organized as a group and identified with the struggle for a Jewish state. The Palestinian soldiers then brought large numbers of the survivors to Italy in order to facilitate illegal immigration to the Land of Israel. They stayed in Europe until 1946 and participated actively both in the Brichah and in Aliyah Bet.

The *shlichim* were all members of the Hagana, the Yishuv's main underground movement. The Yishuv as a whole had been organizing itself during 1943-5 for a decisive showdown over its future. The British connection was considered an inevitable fact of life, but a pro-Zionist solution at the end of the world war would probably entail a confrontation with the Arab states, and an anti-Zionist solution might necessitate a major political, and possibly even a military, struggle against Britain herself. Great Britain was defined – by Moshe Sneh, head of the Hagana, in an article in *Ha'aretz* in October 1944 – as a 'bad partner.' She would remain a partner, but political and military pressure might be needed to turn her into a 'good' one. It is therefore not surprising that in the wake of the British anti-Zionist decision of September 1945, the Hagana and the underground groups, IZL and LHY, joined forces to fight the British in a movement called Tnuat Hameri (Resistance Movement), although the name was originally intended for the Hagana in its new activist guise.

By participating in Tnuat Hameri,[34] each of the three organizations sought to achieve different goals. The Hagana (40,000 members in 1946) had no policy of its own. It executed the orders it received from the Jewish Agency, and especially from Ben-Gurion and Moshe Sharett, whose policy was still to pressure the British by making them recognize the Yishuv's ability to foil any anti-Zionist solution. The IZL (Irgun Zvai Leumi or Etzel), which numbered about 1,500 men, of whom 300 were active fighters, decided to continue the 'war' it had already declared against the British in 1944, in order to bring about a massive Jewish revolt against the British in Palestine. The LHY, or Stern group (120 fighters out of a force of 300) wished, more grandly, to drive British imperialism out of the Middle East.

Tnuat Hameri functioned until the so-called Black Sabbath of 29 June 1946, when the British rounded up the leaders of the Jewish Agency and several thousand Hagana members in an attempt to smash the latter organization. Contrary to the later contentions of the Hagana leaders, it was precisely this action which indeed broke the will of the majority of the leaders of the

Jewish Agency to continue armed actions against Britain. The leadership, which met in Paris in August 1946, agreed to put a halt to the armed struggle against the British; this remained in effect until the War of Independence in 1948. Their activities in support of illegal immigration, a field in which the Hagana had been active before, did continue, however, even more energetically.

In July, Tnuat Hameri was broken up when the leadership of the Hagana disavowed an IZL action directed against the British administration's offices located in the King David Hotel in Jerusalem. Hagana had agreed to the action, but the explosion in the hotel killed more than ninety persons – British, Arabs, and Jews – because a warning telephoned to the British Secretary of the Palestine administration had not been transmitted to the people in the building. Hagana publicly denounced the action and Tnuat Hameri ceased to exist.

From the Black Sabbath until the end of 1947, only IZL and LHY were militarily active in Palestine. To the extent that military actions during this period had any influence on the political outcome, credit must go to these two organizations. Hagana had previously concentrated its attention on those aspects of the struggle against the British which were most effective internationally, and this tendency intensified after the Black Sabbath. First and foremost among these policies was that of fostering illegal immigration, Aliyah Bet, which registered success after success. From the end of World War II until the declaration of the State, 69,000 immigrants reached Palestine or the Cyprus detention camps.

The British, on their part, reached a dead end in their dealings with the Jewish Agency after their action against the Hagana. In desperation, they began to expel illegal immigrants to camps in Cyprus in August 1946. Illegal immigration was most troublesome for the Mandate government because the actions taken to deal with it put the administration in a bad light in the eyes of public opinion in America, Europe, and even in Britain. Although, for the most part, the British public supported their government's Palestine policy, most European nations saw the Jewish struggle favourably, thus increasing Britain's diplomatic difficulties. And, as we know, the British government was forced to face America's recurring demands for the entry of the 100,000 refugees.

An impasse had been reached in the summer of 1946. Relationships between Jews and British had reached an unprecedented low. Truman had already rejected the proposals submitted by the British in the wake of the Anglo-American Committee's report, which were tantamount to a continuation of the White Paper policy: they would have brought in close to 100,000

Jewish immigrants as a last gesture to the Zionists but no more. In August 1946 there was a definite possibility that the U.S. might give up its attempt to influence British policy altogether, because there was nothing very specific that the Americans could propose regarding the future of Palestine. In essence, the British still wanted an Arab Palestine with guaranteed rights for a permanent Jewish minority under British protection. The Zionists demanded freedom of immigration and a Jewish administration of the country. The Arabs wanted a clearly Arab state in treaty relations with Britain. The unequivocal American demand for the immigration of 100,000 now seemed unrelated to anything on the agenda.

American indifference could have meant disaster for the Zionists. They might then have had to face the overwhelming military might of Britain and the steadfast opposition of Arabs with no real political allies. On top of everything else, the Kielce pogrom had just caused the flooding of the DP camps with Jewish refugees from the east. In the light of these circumstances, the Zionist leadership took decisive political action. At their meeting in Paris early in August 1946, the Jewish Agency executive decided to accept a reasonable partition plan, if one were offered. Practically speaking, this meant that the partition of Palestine now became the goal of the Zionist movement, and the Biltmore resolutions which called for a Jewish state in all of western Palestine were abandoned.

The abandonment of the Biltmore program did not come easily to the Jewish Agency. But the mass of refugees streaming into the DP camps was being demoralized through inactivity and Ben-Gurion, again, feared that they would opt for Western countries. The historic opportunity of realizing the goal of an autonomous Jewish political existence in Palestine might thus be lost. Leaders supporting the Biltmore program in principle, such as Rabbi Yehuda L. Maimon of the Mizrahi or Stephen S. Wise of America, thus grew reconciled to statism through partition as the only way to salvage something of what they had to this point been advocating.

The person who transformed the Agency decision in Paris into a political factor of real importance was undoubtedly Dr Nahum Goldman. He brought the new decision to the attention of the American government, and apparently succeeded in impressing several key members of the administration, notably Deputy Secretary Dean Acheson and War Secretary Robert P. Patterson, with the prospects opened up by the Jewish Agency's proposal. The American government finally was inclined to view partition as a way out of the morass, and subsequently the American Jewish Committee, too, lent its support to this solution. The AJC had previously declared that it would not back the proposal unless the U.S. government did so as well.

On the eve of Yom Kippur 5707 (October 1946), President Truman published a statement which inadvertently became a historic declaration. He stated that if a compromise were reached between the Agency's new proposal and the British position, American public opinion would support such a solution. This lukewarm statement, which had more negative than positive elements from a Zionist viewpoint, was misinterpreted both by the American press and by the British government. Despite its careful phrasing by the State Department, it was taken to mean that the American government now supported partition.

The interpretation in London of Truman's policy statement was crucial. The British thought they were faced with an American administration that was under Jewish influence and could not be moved from an unrealistically pro-Zionist position. They believed that they could give in neither to the demand for increased Jewish immigration nor to the demand for any kind of Jewish state. On the other hand, they certainly could not afford a hostile confrontation with the U.S. on this issue, which was, after all, only a secondary matter in Anglo-American relations. The only way out of the impasse for Britain seemed to be to turn the whole matter of Palestine over to the United Nations. There the British hoped to obtain international support for their line of action by threatening to leave Palestine unless their proposals for a solution were adopted.

It should perhaps be emphasized that while the British were probably beginning to play with the idea of withdrawing from Palestine in the fall of 1946, they were still very much hoping to have their way at the UN. Nor was this hope without substance. Anti-Zionist Russia could hardly favour a Jewish state. Latin American countries would probably take into account the Vatican's dislike of the idea of Jewish sovereignty in Palestine. Western Europe was traditionally pro-British and would probably not voice opposition to British policy in the Middle East.

Nor were Zionist leaders, by and large, eager to see the British go. At least some feared the unknown powers that would take the British place: it would be best to find a solution for Jewish statehood in Palestine within the framework of the British Empire. As late as March 1947, at Sandhurst, Abba Eban spoke of ensuring British imperial interests within the boundaries of the future Jewish state in return for close ties and, indeed, protection by Britain for the Jews. Some Zionist leaders were clearly clutching at straws, because it should have been apparent by that time that the British had long since made their decision to support Arab nationalism rather than the Zionist movement.

In 1947, the struggle for the future of Palestine was waged at the UN. British hopes for a solution on the lines of a British-protected Arab Palestine were

shattered by a number of developments that reflected new postwar align-
ments. Public opinion in western Europe had been decisively influenced by
the Jewish struggle for immigration into Palestine, and had become overwhelmingly pro-Zionist. In April 1947, Russia made it clear that she preferred independent states to the continuation of British rule in Palestine. Vatican influence was no longer the only decisive element in the Palestine policies
of the Latin American governments. Nor was the Vatican stand on Palestine
quite clear – provided Jerusalem was internationalized, and the holy places
open to access, the Vatican would not intervene. The Latin Americans therefore decided on their attitude to the Palestine problem without reference to
Church pressures. The stage was now set for the decision, in November 1947,
to partition Palestine. The Israeli War of Independence followed.

How was the emergence from powerlessness achieved? What made the
British go to the UN? The decisive influence was American pressure which
prevented Britain from implementing her anti-Zionist policy. America's pressure in turn was motivated by the presence of the Holocaust survivors in the
DP camps. This pressure was kept up on American decision-makers by American Jewry, cultivating a receptive American public. So the establishment of
the State of Israel and the consequent achievement of a political power base
for the Jewish people was made possible, to a large degree, by the Jews in the
Diaspora: the survivors who organized groups like the Brichah, and American Jewry. This corrects the impression that the main factor leading to statehood was the activity of the Jewish underground movements in Palestine. All
these developments, of course, had built on the fundamental contribution of
the prewar Zionist movement – the building up of the Yishuv by three generations of Zionist immigrants.

There is no doubt that the influence of organized Holocaust survivors, and
of the American pressure which was related to their problem, set the stage for
the Zionists' diplomatic triumph. A second influential factor was Aliyah Bet
– 'illegal immigration' – and the favourable public opinion which it generated while creating grave diplomatic difficulties for Britain. Aliyah Bet was
led by Palestinian Jews; but again, the people who dared to board the dangerous old boats and brave the British Navy's patrols in the Mediterranean
were, most of them, the Holocaust survivors from the DP camps. It was they,
who by their perseverance and courage influenced political decisions in Great
Britain and America, and contributed their share to the establishment of Israel.

A third factor was indeed the underground movements, although they
influenced British decisions considerably less than they tried to make out

after 1948.[35] But they did bother the British, kept the Palestine problem continually in the headlines of newspapers and the political calculations of governments, and made British administration in Palestine very difficult. The IZL failed in its attempts to cause a Jewish uprising in Palestine. Had it succeeded, there is little doubt that the overwhelming might of the British Army would have quelled the rebellion and caused untold harm to the nascent Jewish power base. However, Hagana shrewdly dissociated itself from IZL and LHY, and the impression was gained abroad that the majority of the Yishuv was opposed to their tactics. This posture prevented armed British action against the whole Yishuv: the British public would not have stood for massive intervention to handle 'a few terrorists,' especially not so soon after the Holocaust. Unable therefore to use overt military means on a large scale, the British Army and police in Palestine proved powerless to defeat the two 'dissident' organizations. Yet the pinpricks they suffered at the hands of the underground caused them to act with haste and frustration until they threw the whole problem to the UN.

The paralysis of the Arab national movement because of the alliance of its leaders with the Nazis, and the support by the Soviets of the Jewish exodus from eastern Europe, motivated by the desire to weaken the British position in the Middle East, were also contributory factors. Was the State of Israel history's answer, or to put it in an even more vulgar way, the reward the Jewish people received for the murder of its sons and daughters during the Holocaust? This is emphatically *not* the conclusion of our investigation. Rather, what seems to emerge is that the Holocaust had an important escalating influence on the attitudes and actions of Jewish political bodies generally, and on those of the Yishuv in particular. Thus, the IZL started its military activities against the British in early 1944 under the impact of the news of the murder of European Jewry. Hagana operations and illegal immigration were also largely influenced by the impact of the European disaster on Hagana members. But the most direct, immediate influence of the Holocaust was that exercised by the survivors themselves on the political developments that led to the establishment of Israel. They made Britain's pro-Arab policies impossible, and earned the sympathy and support of people everywhere. They also contributed significantly to the parallel formation of a Jewish power bloc in the United States. While it is true to say that the actual war for Israel's independence, from 1947 to 1949, was fought largely by the sons and daughters of the small Yishuv who were subsequently joined by some of the European DPs, it must be concluded that the securing of the State of Israel, the emergence from powerlessness, was to a large degree the direct result of the dynamics within the Jewish world as a whole which the Holocaust set in motion. Relative Jewish power is thus intimately connected with its former almost absolute absence.

Notes

FOREWORD

1 In a 1919 letter Hitler wrote: 'Antisemitism arising out of purely emotional causes finds its ultimate expression in pogroms. Rational antisemitism must be directed toward a methodical legal struggle ... The final aim must be the deliberate removal of the Jews.'

2 See Joseph B. Schechtman, *The Mufti and the Führer*, New York 1965, especially pp. 151, 157 ff.

3 Deborah E. Lipstadt has discovered that in 1938 49 per cent of persons polled in the United States believed that European Jews deserved the treatment they were receiving from the Nazis. (*AJS Newsletter*, June 1977, p. 20).

4 See Henry Feingold, *The Politics of Rescue*, New Brunswick, N.J., 1970, p. 199, also pp. 183, 206, 254.

5 J.P. Sartre, *Antisemite and Jew*, New York 1948, p. 54. Sartre's otherwise profound account lapses into the 'scapegoat theory' at this one point.

6 *The Destruction of the European Jews*, Chicago 1961, p.v. Every other account of the Holocaust is indebted to this masterful work.

7 Arnold Toynbee in his debate with Yaacav Herzog. See Herzog, *A People That Dwells Alone*, London 1975, p. 31.

8 See Henry Friedlander, *On the Holocaust: A Critique of the Treatment of the Holocaust in History Textbooks* ... New York 1973.

9 Bruno Bettelheim lapsed into the suggestion that Anne Frank's family could and should have acquired 'a gun or two' and gone down fighting. This absurd suggestion must be distinguished from his fair criticism of the Anne Frank *play*, and in particular of its end – Anne's statement of her belief in the goodness of man. *The Informed Heart*, Glencoe 1960, p. 254

10 See Franklin Littell, *The Crucifixion of the Jews*, New York 1975.

11 *Negative Dialektik*, Frankfurt a/M 1975, pp. 354 ff.
12 W.R. Beyer, *Vier Kritiken* Cologne 1970 pp. 190 ff.
13 *Ibid.*
14 See e.g. K.D. Bracher, *The German Dictatorship*, New York 1971.
15 On this theme see also Terence Des Pres, *The Survivor*, New York 1976. The work of a non-Jewish author, this book focuses on the universal significance of the testimony, and emphasizes this still further by including the Soviet slave labour camp in its scope.

I RESCUE BY NEGOTIATIONS?

1 Helmut Krausnick, 'Judenverfolgungen' in: Hans Buchheim, et al., *Anatomie des SS Staates*, Olten und Freiburg 1965, vol. 2, pp. 360 ff.
2 Hans Habe, *The Mission*, New York 1967
3 Yehuda Bauer, *My Brother's Keeper*, Philadelphia 1974, pp. 274-6
4 Henry L. Feingold, *The Politics of Rescue*, New Brunswick, N.J., 1970; Saul S. Friedman, *No Haven for the Oppressed*, Detroit 1973; David S. Wyman, *Paper Walls*, Amherst, Mass., 1968
5 Lucy S. Davidowicz, *The War Against the Jews*, Philadelphia 1975
6 Josep Ackermann, *Himmler als Ideologe*, Goettingen 1970; Norman Rich, *Hitler's War Aims*, New York 1973; Alois Hilgruber, *Die Endloesung und das deutsche Ostimperium*, in *Vierteljahreshefte fuer Zeitgeschichte 1972*, Heft 2, pp. 133-53; Joachim C. Fest, *Hitler*, New York 1975
7 Raul Hilberg, *The Destruction of the European Jews*, Chicago 1961, p. 467
8 Wisliceny's testimony, 11/18/46, Trial Proceedings, Onlud 17/46, p. 132, quoted in Livia Rothkirchen, *Churban Yahadut Slovakia*, Jerusalem 1961, p. 243
9 M.B.D. Weissmandel, *Min Hametzar*, New York 1953, p. 45
10 *Ibid.*, p. 66
11 For a detailed account see my *Holocaust in Historical Perspective*, Seattle 1978.
12 Public Record Office, JR (44) 18, 5/31/44; 6/28/44; and U.S. Foreign Relations, 1944, vol. 1, p. 1074
13 *Ibid.*, p. 1047, p. 1061; and State Department paper 840.48 Refugees/6-944; PRO – Jr (44), 7/1/44
14 Shalom Rosenfeld, ed., *Tik Plili 124*, Tel-Aviv 1956, pp. 76-89
15 *Ibid.*
16 U.S. Foreign Relations, 1944, vol. 1, p. 537
17 See Bela Vago, 'The Intelligence Aspect of the Joel Brand Mission' in *Yad Vashem Studies*, vol. 10, Jerusalem, 1975
18 Heinz Hoehne, *The Order of the Death's Head*, London 1969, pp. 483-539
19 WRB cable 2867, WRB Archive, Roosevelt Library, Hyde Park, New York

Notes 81

20 Randolph L. Braham, ed., *The Destruction of Hungarian Jewry*, New York 1963, docs. 214, 294, 295
21 *Supra*, n. 18
22 Interview with Roswell D. McClelland, 7/13/67 OHD, Institute of Contemporary Jewry, Hebrew University; Rudolf Kasztner, *Bericht*, Munich, 1961, pp. 211-16
23 Braham, *The Destruction of Hungarian Jewry*, vol. 2, p. 700
24 Yad Vashem, 0-51/DN – 39/2119

2 FORMS OF JEWISH RESISTANCE DURING THE HOLOCAUST

1 Henri Michel, *The Shadow War*, London 1965, p. 247
2 For other definitions of 'resistance' see *Jewish Resistance During the Holocaust*, Jerusalem 1971, especially the contributions of Yahil, Blumenthal, and Zuckermann.
3 Shmuel Krakowsky, *Jewish Resistance in Poland* Jerusalem 1977
4 Ireneusz Caban and Zygmunt Mankowski, *Zwiazek Walki Zbrojnej i Armia Krajowa w okregu Lubelskim, 1939–1944*, vol. 2, Lublin 1968, pp. 504-5
5 Moreshet Archive, D. 331
6 Abba Kovner, in a paper to the conference, 'Holocaust – A Generation After,' March 1975, New York; to be published in 1980
7 Shalom Cholawski, *Ir Vaya'ar Bamatzor*, Tel-Aviv 1974, and 'Armed Jewish Resistance in West Byelorussian Ghettoes,' PHD thesis, Hebrew University, 1978
8 Artur Eisenbach, *Hitlerowska Politika Zaglady Zydow*, Warsaw 1961, pp. 228-9
9 Jacob Sloan, ed., *Notes From the Warsaw Ghetto: the Journal of Emmanuel Ringelblum*, New York 1958, p. 47
10 Yad Vashem, AJDC Krakow, 345-145, Bericht fuer's erste Halbjahr 1942
11 Nili Keren Patkin, *OSE Rescue Operations in France, 1939–1944*, unpublished MA thesis, Institute of Contemporary Jewry, Jerusalem 1975
12 Aharon Weiss, 'Ledarkam shel Ha'Judenratim bidrom-mizrach Polin,' in *Yalkut Moreshet*, no. 15, 1972, p. 98

3 ZIONISM, THE HOLOCAUST, AND THE ROAD TO ISRAEL

1 Simon Dubnow, *Geschichte des Juedischen Volkes*, Berlin 1926-9, vol. 3, pp. 267-72; vol. 4, p. 433; vol. 7, pp. 64 ff.
2 See Shmuel Ettinger, 'Shorshei Ha'antishemiut Bazman Hehadash,' in: *Molad*, 1969, vol. 2, no. 9, pp. 323-40; Uriel Tal, *Yahadut Venatzrut Ba'Reich Hasheni*, Jerusalem 1970, esp. pp. 205-24; George L. Mosse, *Germans and Jews*, London 1971, esp. pp. 34-60.

3 Dubnow, *Geschichte*, vol. 9, pp. 305-16

4 See Tal, *Yahadut*, Ya'kov Katz, 'Yihuda shel Yahadut Hungaria,' in *Hanhagat Yehudei Hungaria Bemivhan Ha'Shoa*, Jerusalem 1976; E.D. Wynot, 'A Necessary Cruelty – The Emergence of Official Anti-Semitism in Poland, 1936–1939,' in *American Historical Review*, vol. 76 (1975), pp. 1035-58.

5 See Raphael Mahler, *Yehudei Polin bein Shtei Milhamot Ha'olam*, Tel-Aviv 1969; also my book, *My Brother's Keeper*, Philadelphia 1974.

6 Emil Fackenheim, 'The Jewish People Return to History,' in *General Assembly Papers*, Council of Jewish Federations and Welfare Funds, New York 1975

7 See *Hitlers Zweites Buch*, Stuttgart 1961, pp. 64, 153-8, 174-5, 220 ff.

8 The Bund was founded in 1897 in Czarist Russia, and in the early years of this century developed a radical socialist ideology closely akin to that of the Russian Mensheviks. The Folkists (Folks-Partei) were established by the historian Simon Dubnow in 1906; their originally rather considerable influence waned in the thirties in Poland. The Territorialist movement began when an important minority of Zionists left the Zionist Organization in 1905 in protest against the rejection of Herzl's idea to establish a temporary Jewish settlement in Uganda, and founded the Jewish Territorialist Association under the leadership of Israel Zangwill. Under the pressure of the developing tragedy of Jewish flight from Germany and Poland, the Freiland (Freeland) League was set up in Britain in 1935, dedicated to finding a territory for the settlement of Jews. Agudat Israel was founded in Kattowitz (then Germany) in 1912 as the political organ of anti-Zionist orthodoxy.

9 See Bauer, *My Brother's Keeper*, pp. 57-104.

10 The territory was set aside for Jewish settlement in 1928, and declared a Jewish autonomous region in 1934.

11 See Israel Gutman, *The Jews of Warsaw*, Jerusalem 1977.

12 For a modern definition of Zionism, see Walter Laqueur, *A History of Zionism*, New York 1976, esp. pp. 589-99; and Yigal Elam, *Mavo Lehistoria Zionist Aheret*, Tel-Aviv 1974.

13 In the late years of the nineteenth century there were 457,592 inhabitants in Palestine, of whom 60,000 were Jews, according to Vital Cuinet, *Liban et Syrie, Geographie administrative statistique, descriptive et raisonée*, Paris 1896. The figure of 300,000 is quoted in: *Palestine, A Study of Jewish, Arab, and British Policies*, New York 1947, p. 463

14 See Isaiah Friedman, *The Question of Palestine, 1914–1918*, London 1973.

15 Leonard Stein, *The Balfour Declaration*, London 1961, p. 394

16 See *Memoranda Prepared by the Government of Palestine*, London 1937, Colonial no. 137, p. 37. Of the 664 successful claimants, 387 were resettled, whereas the others allowed their claims to lapse, presumably because they found other, perhaps

better, employment. The numbers of illegal Arab immigrants, referred to in the subsequent paragraph in the text, can perhaps be guessed from the official statistics which indicate that between 1922 and 1942 the Moslem population increased from 589,177 to 995,292 (by over 68 per cent); this would indicate a large-scale immigration, even assuming a very large natural increase. Officially registered Arab illegals who stayed in the country, between 1933 and 1939, numbered 13,574. Another 10,145 were deported.

17 See Chaim Weizmann's two articles on the solution of the Palestine problem and the Jews, in the *New York Times*, 13 August 1941 and in *Foreign Affairs*, January 1942.

18 See John Marlowe, *Rebellion in Palestine*, London 1946, pp. 209-210, 213.

19 Yehuda Bauer, *From Diplomacy to Resistance*, New York 1973, pp. 25-33

20 Saul S. Friedman, *No Haven for the Oppressed*, Detroit 1973

21 This attitude was very prevalent among Jewish leaders. See for instance Naomi Cohen, *Not Free to Desist*, Philadelphia 1972, for the attitudes of the American Jewish Committee; see also Bauer, *My Brother's Keeper*, for the attitude of the JDC leadership.

22 Henry L. Feingold, *The Politics of Rescue*, New Brunswick, N.J., 1970, pp. 22-44; Bauer, *My Brother's Keeper*, pp. 231-6

23 Feingold, in *Politics of Rescue*, pp. 239 ff., put a different interpretation on the establishment of the Board. He believed that Morgenthau was a prime mover in the developments. The records of the WRB at Hyde Park, New York, seem to me to indicate that Morgenthau needed a great deal of convincing by his non-Jewish assistants, John W. Pehle, Josiah E. DuBois jr., and Randolph Paul. See also the *Morgenthau Diaries* edited by John Blum, Boston 1967, vol. 2., p. 209 ff; and Arthur D. Morse, *While Six Million Died*, New York 1967, p. 71

24 See Samuel Halperin, *The Political World of American Zionism*, Detroit 1961.

25 See Lawrence H. Fuchs, 'American Jews and the Presidential Vote,' in L.H. Fuchs, *American Ethnic Policies*, New York 1968; also John G. Snetsinger, 'Truman and the Creation of Israel,' (unpublished dissertation, Ann Arbor, Michigan, 1974). I am greatly indebted to my colleague, Professor Moshe Davis, for information regarding these and the Holy Land aspects, which are part of a major research undertaken by him and others.

26 British archives have been opened up to 1947. American sources have become available in part through the publication of the Foreign Relations of the U.S. volumes for 1947 and 1948. However, much of the detailed research still remains to be done. Zionist and Israeli archives for 1947-8 are closed, as of 1977.

27 See Bauer, *From Diplomacy to Resistance*, pp. 234-52.

28 Aryeh Morgenstern, 'Va'ad Hahatzalah Hameuhad shel'yad Hasohnut Hayehudit, 1943-1945,' in: *Yalkut Moreshet 13*, 1971, pp. 60-103

29 Yehuda Bauer, *Flight and Rescue: Brichah*, New York 1970

30 Abba Kovner, 'Shlihutam shel Ha'ahronim (Di Shliches fun di Letzte),' in *Yalkut Moreshet 16*, 1973, p. 36. This very important statement was presented in English to a conference on the Holocaust in New York, in March 1975, and is scheduled to appear in print shortly.

31 For details, see Bauer, *Flight and Rescue.*

32 Central Zionist Archives, Jewish Agency Executive, 21 November 1945

33 I am grateful for Mr Heymont's permission to use his diary.

34 See Yehuda Slutzki, ed., *Sefer Toldot Hahagana*, Tel-Aviv 1972, vol. 3, book 2, chapters 42-3 (pp. 854-905).

35 Here are some examples of the historiography, referred to a number of times in the text, which tends to overemphasize the importance of the Yishuv's underground: *Sefer Toldot Hahagana*; Menahem Begin, *The Revolt*, Jerusalem 1971; David Niv, *Bema'arhot Ha'irgun Ha'tzvai Ha'leumi*, Tel-Aviv 1973, vol. 4; Shmuel Katz, *Yom Ha'esh*, Tel-Aviv 1966.

Index